Who Killed Honor Bright?

How William Butler and George Yeats Caused the Fall of the Irish Free State

© **Patricia Hughes.**

ISBN 9781909275072 Paperback; 9781909275027 Hardback; 9781909275010 ePub

Third Edition

Hues Books Ltd 2014

'William Butler Yeats and Honor Bright' Series:

1.   W. B. Yeats and the Murder of Honor Bright

2.   An Analysis of Selected Poetry by William Butler Yeats between 1918 and 1928

3.   Who Killed Honor Bright?
    How William Butler and George Yeats Caused the Fall of the Irish Free State

This book is a tribute to my father, who never resembled a prostitute's son, and to my grandmother, who never was a prostitute. It is dedicated to their whole 'clan'.

Title page photograph:
The corpse of Honor Bright / Lily O'Neill photographed by Garda Sgt. A. Gordon at Ticknock crossroads, County Dublin early in the morning of 9th June 1925.

Front cover: William Butler Yeats in 1923 aged 57.
Back cover: Kevin Barry O'Neill in 1943 aged 22.

Table of Contents

ISBN 978-1-909275-02-7	2
Introduction	5
A Buddha, hand at rest, hand lifted up that blest…	9
A Sphinx with woman breast and lion paw	34
And right between these two a girl at play…	52
The Three Old Rascals	72
The Tyrants That Spat	82
The Falsified Witness Deposition	90
The Bullet	95
The Assassin	96
The Foster-MotherError! Bookmark not defined.	
Mrs McGill's partner	98
Garda Photographs of Lily O'Neill/Honor Bright	99
Oedipus' Child Descends into the Loveless Dust	124
Ruin, Wreck and Wrack	150
'Legendary' Honor Bright	163
Bibliography	174
Notes	180

Introduction

This factual book focuses on the death of Honor Bright in Ireland in 1925 and reveals how authorities in the Irish Free State harrassed and then murdered her. Afterwards she was maligned as a prostitute and her assassin acquitted. It portrays corruption and a lack of legal restraint at the heart of the new government.

The newly established Garda Síochana was used to spread deceitful rumours and coerce witnesses in order to conceal the victim's real identity and the reason for her death. False evidence, perjury and the forceful suppression of potential witnesses at a sham trial led to huge public demonstrations, but newspapers were coerced into printing only authorised stories or facing the consequences from the Garda and the Minister of Justice.

All persons involved in these events systematically destroyed evidence, or else hid it from prying eyes. Therefore the evidence provided in this book is almost all circumstantial. However the lives of William Butler (WB) Yeats, his wife George Yeats, Minister of Justice Kevin O'Higgins, Commissioner Eoin O'Duffy, Chief Superintendent David Neligan, Lily O'Neill or Honor Bright and Kevin O'Neill have never before been juxtaposed. Examined together they reveal a huge amount of new data that confirms my conclusions.

Public appearances of those involved in this political scandal became very dangerous; some were killed and many fled. Voters became very aware that the government was unaccountable, so from 1925 political support moved quickly away from a unionist free state towards an independent republic. Eamon de Valera's first action on taking office as President of the Republic in 1932 was to dismantle the remains of the previous government; in particular he sacked Eoin O'Duffy as Commissioner of the Garda. The Yeats family had moved out of Ireland by then, and O'Higgins had been assassinated.

In 2006 in The Guardian I came across a picture that my father, Kevin O'Neill, had shown me as a child. It was of W. B. Yeats receiving the Nobel Prize, and I remembered noticing his likeness to my father.

There was a dense cloud of obscurity around my grandmother. My father possessed hardly anything to do with her: two brief newspaper articles, the bullet that had killed her and the police photographs of her corpse that he had brought back from Dublin. My search for her began in register offices, but I didn't know her name: Honor Bright was a pseudonym, but was she Lily or Lizzie O'Neill? After looking again and again I couldn't find either, but I knew that she came from Carlow.

Though it sounded like a mystery novel it was an actual murder, so I wrote to the Garda Archives in Dublin Castle. Initially the officer in charge was helpful, but he was soon moved from the post. On the Internet and trawling through record offices, newspapers, archives, literature and biographies uncovered lots of detail which, when transposed with the poetry of Yeats and biographies of him and of his wife, created a new landscape. It made me certain, after many revisions, that my facts are correct. A DNA test would have proved it conclusively but, though my brother still offers to provide a Y chromosome, no Yeats descendants have yet replied to my requests to my potential family.

What is my motivation? My father was distressed on returning from visiting Dublin in 1966, when he had asked the Garda about his mother's murder. They had shown him their case archive (as the case is still open) and given him the bullet and photographs as he had no other picture of her, but strongly advised him that she was a rampant prostitute, so it was best not to uncover old wounds. Upon his return he cried for three days before showing us what he had found. Afterwards he stopped trying to find out about his mother, anxious about the effect on his wife and daughters.

The modern Garda and the Minister of Justice in the Republic of Ireland have deflected every effort made to open the Honor Bright murder case file. No doubt this was partly because of their own force's involvement, and partly because Yeats has become a lucrative symbol of Irish national culture since then, so that they did not wish to stain his reputation. However the culpability of a previous Garda Chief Superintendent acting under the authority of a former Minister of Justice cannot be evaded.

Honor Bright's story will explain Yeats's poetry to those who consider it difficult.

Shortly before he died I asked my father if he had done everything he had wanted to do in life; he answered that he had always intended to write a book about his parentage. So this is a tribute to him, Kevin O'Neill, who never in the slightest way resembled a prostitute's son, and also to my grandmother Lily O'Neill, who never was a prostitute. I want to set the record straight for all generations of my family, including even my errant grandfather William Butler Yeats. I dedicate this book to the whole 'clan'.

My thanks to my late husband Paul for showing me the way; the National Archives in Ireland for providing documents, countless other librarians and archivists and Breeda MacDonald and Kevin Barry for helping with my research. Thousands of people on LinkedIn, Academia.edu, Twitter, Goodreads and Facebook endorsed me, including amongst others genealogists, historians, politicians and students of literature, and I'm eternally thankful for their goodwill. I am particularly indebted to my family and friends who found evidence and encouraged me.

Poems in this book are by William Butler Yeats, from the volume edited by Daniel Albright. Most of Yeats's poetry from 1918 was either written about Lily or about his sense of guilt. Some are in the text to support the story of my grandmother, since nothing else remains of her.

Patricia Hughes, May 2015

Postscript
In this third edition there is more evidence, and the Appendices in previous editions have been incorporated into the text. Photographs are more easily accessible, and the print is easier to read.
PH

A Buddha, hand at rest, hand lifted up that blest...

also known as

Willie
William Butler Yeats
Demon est Deus inversus (DEDI)
The Eagle
Dante
The Poet
The Nobel Prize winner
Senator Yeats
The Senator
Michael Robartes
The centaur
A swan
Yeats
Owen Aherne
Hanrahan
An old scarecrow
The Hero
A man young and old
Paris
A sixty-year-old smiling public man
Oedipus

On 13 June 1865 William Butler Yeats was born in Sandymount, a seaside town near Dublin. His father John Butler Yeats was from a family of Church of Ireland clerics, but had taken up law rather than religion. On marrying Susan Pollexfen from Sligo he was a barrister. However he had studied law only to please his parents; upon coming into his wife's dowry he resigned from the bar to become a portraitist and painter, despite the penurious effect this had on his family. Two sisters - Susan and Elizabeth (Lily and Lolly) - were born after William (Willie), and the youngest was John (Jack). As in Wales, most Irish people had nicknames, e.g. 'Jones the bread', because the same names constantly recurred.

When Willie was two his father began an art course in London, and because there was no income the children were sent for long intervals to their mother's relatives in Sligo. Five years later the Yeats family moved back to Sligo. However after a further two years they moved back to London, where the art scene was livelier and criticism less harsh. Willie, who was now nine years old, started at state school for the first time in his life in Hammersmith; there was no money for a private school, even for the eldest boy. Irish, poor, semi-nomadic and only partly educated (unable to spell), but with an ex-barrister father, a middle-class mother and social aspirations, Willie used innate rhetoric to project a powerful image and hide his anxieties. Meanwhile his father was making friends among local artists, so two years later in 1876 the family moved to better lodgings in London, and Willie moved to a new school.

Nevertheless lack of work and money led the family back to Ireland again in 1880, to Howth rather than Dublin because the countryside was cheaper. Yeats, now fifteen, had to change school again. By now he had learnt to be solitary and self-sufficient because of his clumsiness and defective eyesight as well as the fleeting nature of his friendships. His father had always recited poems to him and he began to write his own verse.

In 1883 the family moved again, this time nearer to the city, and one year later William left school and began to attend Art College in Dublin; he had no wish to go to Trinity College as his father and grandfather had done, and in any case he was not sufficiently qualified. By 1885 he was finding more success as a poet than as an artist, and for the first time he was published in the Dublin University Review. He was now able to make real friends on his own, and at college he befriended people who would influence him all his life. By the age of twenty-two he had published in England as well and was on the way to making a name for himself as a poet of Irish folklore and legend.

At twenty-three Yeats met Maud Gonne. She was English by birth and wealthy. Her father, Thomas, was a captain in the British army, and during part of her childhood the family lived in Ireland, but later, after her father was promoted, Maud was educated in France by a governess. There was also a rich aunt who introduced her to society in Paris. She was barely out of her teens when her father died, and soon afterwards she began a relationship with a right-wing French politician called Lucien Millevoye "... obviously a replacement father figure," according to Yeats scholar Deirdre Toomey. "He was 16 years older than she."

Millevoye was a follower of General Georges Boulanger, a hardline nationalist. Boulangistes planned to recapture the eastern territories of France, Alsace and Lorraine on the German border. Millevoye was anti-German but also anti-British, and strongly encouraged Maud to involve herself in Irish politics, so that she began to support rent strikes and oppose evictions.

On 30 January 1889 in Bedford Park, London, Maud and Yeats met, and he was immediately overwhelmed. Their first topic of conversation was not recorded; it was probably to do with the political situation in Ireland, since both were involved, though Yeats was unionist rather than anti-British like Maud. According to R F Foster, Yeats saw Maud as "majestic, unearthly... Immensely tall, bronze-haired, with a strong profile and beautiful skin ..." and immediately became infatuated with her. It was the start of a friendship that would last half a century.

Less than three weeks before this encounter Maud had given birth in Paris to Georges, the son of Millevoye. Yeats met her again two years later in October 1891 when she arrived in Kingstown[1], on the mail boat bearing the body of Irish politician Charles Parnell. Observers thought her tears were for Parnell, but they were for Georges, who had just died aged two-and-a-half, probably from meningitis. Her tears may also have been for Millevoye since the couple subsequently separated. Maud initially kept Georges secret from Yeats, but when he found out she insisted that he was adopted. "It is surprising how naïve Yeats seems to have been over Gonne's child," Toomey says.

Over the next two years grief-stricken Maud was drawn into occultist and spiritualist worlds, already of deep importance to Yeats. Later in his memoirs he recalled that she repeatedly asked his friends whether reincarnation really took place. George Russell (known as AE) assured her that it was indeed possible.

At that time Maud rented a house in Samois-sur-Seine, southeast of Paris, and when Georges died his coffin was laid there in a white tomb. In late 1893 she contacted Millevoye and asked him to meet her at the tomb. Together they descended the small metal ladder and then had sexual intercourse next to the dead baby's coffin, in the hope of resurrecting him, and perhaps also their relationship. The evidence comes from Yeats in his posthumous memoirs, not published until 1972, after his editor wife had died. He wrote that Maud had told him what had happened. Yeats scholar Warwick Gould says, "I cannot imagine any reason why she would have made the story up. It is too bizarre and too personal. But it accords with what we know of her interest in reincarnation."

Yeats's poem of the same year, never published, was clearly inspired by Maud's grief over her dead son, although when he wrote it Yeats still believed that Maud had adopted Georges. Though not as polished as his later verse, it shows his empathy in realist poetry.

On a Child's Death

You shadowy armies of the dead
Why did you take the starlike head,
The faltering feet, the little hand?
For purple kings are in your band
And there the hearts of poets beat;
Why did you take the faltering feet?
She had much need of some fair thing
To make love spread his quiet wing
Above the tumult of her days
And shut out foolish blame & praise.
She has her squirrel & her birds
But these have no sweet human words
And cannot call her by her name:
Their love is but a woodland flame.
You wealthy armies of the dead
Why did you take the starlike head?
(Reproduced by permission of Caitriona Yeats)

Yeats was determined to contact Georges for Maud, so in the same year he joined Madame Blavatsky's Theosophical Society, but he was soon excommunicated for being too forthright. He therefore co-founded the Hermetic Order of the Golden Dawn originally for Maud, and began conducting semi-religious gatherings, séances and rituals. Yeats was obviously still infatuated or 'in love with' Maud, but their love was purely platonic since she was still preoccupied by her past relationships. Meanwhile another member of the Golden Dawn was Florence Farr Emery, with whom he had an affair that carried on for a year; both were influenced by Indian religious practices and astrology, and both were enthralled by the stage and poetry. Like Maud, Florence was an affluent English married woman, but in those days of marriage for money, adultery was an acceptable practice among the middle and upper classes, if kept under wraps. Yeats was choosing his friends and lovers with high society and finance in mind, since he was short of such resources.

In 1896 he met Lady Augusta Gregory, an affluent widow whose objective was to institute an Irish national theatre. Yeats became her main literary focus; she subsequently invited him to her stately home, Coole Park, every summer for three decades, feeding him food, sympathy, inspiration, finance and friendship in equal amounts. In effect, she became his literary mentor and ersatz mother. She also gave him responsibility for re-establishing cultural nationalism in her Irish national theatre, which appealed greatly to his non-violent ideal of unification of the north and south, of Protestants and Catholics. So by the early years of the twentieth century he had become manager and artistic director of the Abbey Theatre.

Also in 1896 Yeats had an affair with Olivia Shakespear, another wealthy married upper class Englishwoman, just like Florence and Maud, and another daughter of a retired senior army officer, again just like Maud. Olivia was around his age and trying to be a writer in London (though her novels were unsuccessful), and she collaborated with his former lover, Florence Farr Emery, in writing two plays. In 1885 Olivia had married a senior lawyer, and the following year had given birth to their only child, Dorothy. The affair with Yeats began ten years later and was over again in one year, but they remained friends, as Yeats usually did with past mistresses. Of course, such affairs were not publicly acknowledged since there existed a much stricter code of conduct for religious people and the working class.

Members of the Golden Dawn, established principally by Yeats for Maud, believed in one fundamental religion and one fundamental God, despite His myriad identities in different cultures. Members used occult and the paranormal along with rituals based on tarot, Ouija boards and freemasonry. Men and women held equal status. It was a secret society with many influential members in the world of arts, but as it grew problems developed involving goals and objectives. Disputes ultimately led to Yeats resigning from his central role in 1901, though he remained a member.

In 1903 "Yeats stood aghast, angry as well as very miserable..."[2] because of Maud Gonne's marriage to John MacBride, a nationalist military man who founded the radical Irish Brigade, He had been impressed by Maud's involvement in anti-British campaigns.

Yeats, averse to disruption and violence, thought this marriage was madness because of MacBride's inflammatory character and raucous political activity. But he had insufficient financial resources to be her suitor.

"In 1903 [Maud] gave birth to Seán, her son by MacBride. The marriage was short-lived, however, ending bitterly when Maud filed for divorce on the basis of MacBride's alleged debauchery and adultery. The acrimonious trial that ensued was front-page news, both in Ireland and in mainland Europe, with the French courts eventually ruling that due to MacBride's Irish citizenship, and the illegality of divorce in that country, Maud's petition for divorce could not be granted. Instead, she was allowed a legal separation that left her bitter, and for over a decade after, a virtual prisoner in France, as she feared that the legal custody of her son Seán, as granted her by the French courts, would not be honored in Ireland where MacBride resided."[3]

Whether she wanted to marry Yeats is questionable in any case, as their politics were by now far removed from one another. Maud had become determined to defeat the British occupation of Ireland, while Yeats was much more interested in his literary public.

At the time Yeats was 42. The Augustus John portrait of him in the same year, now in Birmingham Art Gallery, shows a sociable man in full bloom. His lifestyle emphasised his freedom: "A note of a typical day in Dublin runs as follows: "Breakfast 10.45; 11 - 1.10 reading script for the theatre and letters; evening Abbey." Yeats was doing everything necessary to keep the Abbey theatre going; he was director, actor and playwright, also in charge of accounts, heating maintenance and other property matters.

In the process he was surrounded by active young actors and actresses. By 1909, according to Joseph Hone's biography of Yeats,"For company in Dublin Yeats depended chiefly on the Arts Club" where "it pleased him to find listeners among the young who were not slaves to paper or to books."[4] Moreover "until he became a member of Stephen's Green Club[5], Yeats stayed when in Dublin at the Nassau Hotel overlooking the College Park." So Yeats was well placed for finding female company, and had the means to entertain. He did not appear to be suffering from unrequited love for Maud.

By now Yeats was a celebrated poet. Up till now his love affairs had always been with affluent English women, usually daughters of senior British Army officers, securely married to respectable men and financially independent. Apart from the fact that they funded him, with such lovers he had no problems to do with pregnancy or marriage and could remain free and independent without family incumbrances.

However his next affair was with Mabel Dickinson, the first exception to this rule. It was the longest affair to date, lasting five years from 1908 to 1913, when he was 43 to 48. She was older and single, an actress and skilled "masseuse"[6]. Though she had a good grasp of literature and drama, she was not upper class or particularly wealthy. She instigated the affair, which was intensely physical despite lacking social or emotional depth. So Hone informs us, "Yeats had formed a liaison with an unmarried woman past her first youth. The liaison, having been carried on for some years without great conviction on either side, had suddenly threatened to land him in difficulties. In the event, it proved that the person concerned harboured no embarrassing designs on him. ... The unfounded suspicion [was] that he had been ensnared by a huntress..."[7]

On June 6th 1913 she claimed that she was pregnant in order to marry him, but this turned out to be untrue. Yeats recoiled in disgust, referring to her as a 'harlot'.[8] Nevertheless the ending of his first affair with an unmarried woman left a four-year gap in his lovelife from 1913 to 1917, as far as we know.

In 1909 his ex-lover Olivia Shakespear had begun hosting a weekly salon in London for writers; she was soon well known as a literary hostess. Shortly afterwards her brother married a member of her circle, Nelly Hyde-Lees, whose daughter was Bertha Georgie. Olivia's new step- niece was approximately the same age as her daughter Dorothy, and the two girls became friends. Georgie was interested in the occult like her mother, and in 1914, aged 22, was introduced to the Hermetic Order of the Golden Dawn by 'Demon est Deus inversus' or 'DEDI', William Butler Yeats. She was bright, sharp and intelligent, but at home she was used to being ignored by her promiscuous maternal relatives and her inebriate father. She took the name 'Nemo sciat', meaning 'no man knows' in Latin, to reflect her love of secrecy and intrigue. But 'nemo' in ancient Greek means fate, destiny or justice, the root of 'nemesis'.

In 1912 Ezra Pound made his way from the United States to England in order to meet Yeats, who was by now widely acknowledged as a great poet. Dorothy and Georgie introduced them to each other at one of Yeats' 'Monday at homes' in his Woburn Buildings flat in London. Soon afterwards Dorothy declared to Georgie that she intended to share her life with Ezra but it had to be kept secret, since her mother would object. Georgie was very good at keeping secrets.

In 1913 after finishing with Mabel Yeats rented Stone Cottage in a remote part of Sussex in order to develop his writing. He hired Ezra, accompanied by Dorothy, as his amanuensis. The two poets became close friends, sharpened their skills and influenced each other greatly. Pound learnt more about poetic structures, while Yeats learnt to compose poems about his contemporary world rather than folk tales and romanticism. From this point forwards, all of Yeats' poetry without exception was concerned with current or personal events, as shown in his famous poem "Easter 1916" about the Easter Uprising, also known as Bloody Sunday. It described those who took part and the forceful British military response, which was sudden, bloody, remorseless and left all Dublin shocked. Many of the Irish nationalist protagonists involved in the uprising were friends of Yeats, but where his endeavours went into literature, theirs had gone into political independence, and they paid for it with their lives. In this poem he named them as people he had trusted: Thomas MacDonagh, Patrick Pearse, Joseph Plunkett and James Connolly. All had been members of the Irish Republican Brotherhood, as he was. Those who did not die in the fighting were captured and sentenced to death by the ruling British courts. The evocative phrase "A terrible beauty is born" caught the hearts and minds of his readership in Ireland and abroad, and turned him overnight into a respected authority on Irish politics. Thereafter certain British politicians occasionally invited Yeats to dinner in London to describe common reaction to political events in the Irish capital.

Nevertheless Yeats was still the same person he had been before, and in Dublin he still inhabited the same upper class world of occult and theatre, poetry and recitals. He was gregarious, happy with all social gatherings and well respected. As he advanced in years he undoubtedly had a deeper understanding of social problems and divisions, and he cared deeply about the whole of Ireland. He had become a recognised Irish poet and was a respected manager of the Irish National Theatre, renowned for his support of Irish literature.

However he had lost contact with the working class, the Catholic majority, and he needed to understand them in order to give valid political opinions. He was not religiously prejudiced or tied to Protestantism; he had good Catholic friends such as Oliver St John Gogarty and Maud, but they were not working class or young. Yeats yearned to absorb the intense political atmosphere in shops, streets, pubs and clubs.

With this in mind he began to revive his childhood existence, walking around Dublin disguised as working class.

With success in public life and advancing years – he was fifty in 1915 - Yeats had to start thinking about what would happen when his father died. John Butler Yeats was becoming very elderly and infirm in New York, and was being kept by his agent, John Quinn, at Yeats's expense. His sisters were unmarried since they had lacked dowries, so Yeats as the potential head of the family had to provide for both of them when his father died. They were both past the change of life, and so was his brother Jack's wife; so only he, the eldest son, was still capable of marrying and producing an heir for the whole Yeats family. Therefore Yeats's bachelor years were quickly replaced by a search for a wife. There were two priorities, wealth and fertility, though the first was more pressing.

With money in mind he approached Maud Gonne. Two decades before she had been his beautiful unrequited love, but she had become a very active politically engaged middle-aged widow, with a raised position in the republican movement for her work with the Dublin working class. By now she was also post-menopausal with grown-up children. During her marriage she had also become Catholic, rather than lapsed Church of Ireland and unionist as he was. She was however still a good middle class friend, with reliable finance and plenty of connections with younger people.

When she refused outright as expected, he immediately approached her daughter Iseult as if by design; perhaps he felt it more tactful to approach the mother first. Iseult was an attractive young woman with access to her mother's fortune, that he would not mind being socially connected to. Nevertheless she also refused immediately, making it kindly but unmistakeably clear that she did not feel any attraction to him.

Olivia Shakespear was another well off, post-menopausal ex-lover with younger relatives. Yeats did not propose to her as she was still married, or to her daughter Dorothy who was currently involved with Ezra. However he was formally introduced to her step-niece in late September 1917 and a quiet wedding followed three weeks later.

After his marriage Yeats needed solitary writing time, so at the start, with his wife's consent, he would retire to the United Arts Club for a day or two. From there he would disguise himself with Abbey Theatre resources and a pseudonym, in order to find out surreptitiously what ordinary people thought and said. He was, after all, a seasoned poet, mage, theatre manager and playwright, so he was used to changing his appearance and putting on a show: in any case he had been practising pretending to be in a different social class since childhood. The world he had grown up in had been full of common people in whose company he had learnt his skills of rhetoric and self-presentation. He was also well used to talking to young women as literary afficionados, actresses or astrological devotees. He simply developed a set of identities that he had invented around 1900, starting with Michael Robartes, a younger, more handsome, sexually active mirror of himself.

In the process of exploring ordinary life he visited dance clubs and paid young women employed there to share one dance with him. At one dance club Yeats met a new woman, so from 1918 he wrote poems about his alter ego and a dancer. In 1918 they got to know each other and fell in love. Yeats became so enamoured that he could not hide his emotions, so George insisted on moving her husband to Oxford, despite having planned, when they married, to live in Dublin.

In 1919 he published The Wild Swans at Coole. Quite suddenly George had become his editor; she began to make a point of not ordering his poems chronologically, so that his poems to his new lover were not easily recognisable. However the reader can see the change in Yeats if s/he examines this volume of poetry chronologically. The earliest poems of 1916-17 are by a mature man grieving for the recently deceased Major Robert Gregory, son of Lady Augusta, and contemplating his own demise:

I have nothing but the embittered sun;
... And now that I have come to fifty years
I must endure the timid sun.

However the tone suddenly changes in 1918 with

Men Improve with the Years:

I am worn out with dreams ...
... all day long I look
Upon this lady's beauty...
Is this my dream or the truth?
O would that we had met
When I had my burning youth!

He has never previously written about his wife's beauty. In fact he thinks it a dream rather than reality because he is not writing about his wife. Yet he wishes for his 'burning youth' because she is young, so he is certainly not talking of middle-aged Maud. He explains in his next poem, The Collar-Bone of a Hare:

... the best thing is

To change my loves while dancing
And pay but a kiss for a kiss.

One can see that he has experience of changing partners in dance clubs. He wishes to 'change his loves' because he has fallen in love with someone other than his wife. He writes in the same amorous mode,

"To A Young Beauty"

Dear fellow-artist, why so free
With every sort of company
With every Jack and Jill?
Choose your companions from the best;
Who draws a bucket with the rest
Soon topples down the hill.

You may, that mirrors for a school,
Be passionate, not bountiful
As common beauties may
Who were not born to keep in trim
With old Ezekiel's cherubim,
But those of Beauvarlet.

I know what wages beauty gives,
How hard a life her servant lives,
Yet praise the winters gone;
There is not a fool can call me friend,
And I may dine at journey's end
With Landor and with Donne.

George may or may not have been a 'young beauty', but she certainly would not have been 'free with every sort of company', having been brought up in exclusive social circles with private tutors, expensive schools and faultless elocution.

She would not have to be urged to 'choose companions from the best'. There would be no reason to think she would ever 'topple down the hill' of society.

However these admonitions would have been appropriate to a dancer in a club; how far could she trust her next dance partner? This young woman is a 'fellow-artist' who 'mirrors for a school', so she sounds like a model living on 'what wages beauty gives'.

His attraction to the dancer showed Yeats being frustrated with his wife. George was twenty-five, upper class, wealthy, rational and determined to maintain the status quo, whereas the dancer was eighteen, working class, intelligent and relatively innocent. Yeats described George as representing 'all things known, all things unknown', while the dancer represented 'all things loved, all things unloved' in "The Double Vision of Michael Robartes".

The contrast between rationality and emotion was very apparent to him in his marriage. George was attempting to have his son and heir as he had wished when they married, but even before she had achieved that, her physical attractions had waned in Yeats's eyes. George's main interest was in controlling her wayward husband in order to preserve her home, just as her promiscuous mother had controlled her alcoholic father. She saw her husband as needing protection from himself, hence her obsession with knowing what he was composing, and with editing all his writings to hide the truth, since he only wrote about reality.

The poem 'Nineteen Hundred and Nineteen' explains how he felt about his wife:

… thereupon

There lurches past, his great eyes without thought,
Under the shadow of stupid straw-pale locks,
That insolent fiend Robert Artisson
To whom the love-lorn Lady Kyteler brought
Bronzed peacock feathers ...

Lady Kyteler was the first woman in Ireland condemned for witchcraft, hundreds of years before. Her sexual partner was her incubus Robert Artisson. Yeats uses these two characters to describe his own relationship, as stupid Robert Artisson, to his wife, as infatuated Lady Kyteler. George had idolized Yeats before their marriage, and had brought him artificial magical tokens, such as occult prowess and languages, which he refers to as 'bronzed peacock feathers'; they did represent hard, intellectual work like bronze mouldings, but not nature, creativity or joy like real peacock feathers. On entering the relationship, her partner had been too stupid to understand how lacking in imagination, how negative and destructive she was.

In this respect her 'automatic writing', begun one day after their hasty marriage and before the couple had learnt to talk to each other honestly, can be recognised as manipulation. It was George's way of convincing her husband that whatever she said had greater wisdom and significance than anything he said. Whether or not it and her 'voices' really did emanate from higher spirits in occult realms, they only made an appearance when she was alone with Yeats, and she was always the channel through which they came, never her husband. Yeats was also a master manipulator however, and would have recognised the motives behind it very soon. This was why he was suddenly tired of '... the old bitter world where they marry in churches...' and felt desperately frustrated, because he was suddenly inhibited, controlled, and no longer able to choose whom he kissed. Nevertheless,

George was still financially and socially important to him.

Probably at his wife's wish, Yeats gave up his rooms in Woburn Buildings in London in June 1919. By then George already knew his new lover's name, because Yeats, unlike her, was incapable of keeping secrets; "I know myself to be utterly indiscreet."[9] Yeats suddenly developed a habit of misspelling his sister's name as 'Lilly' rather than 'Lily', since the latter signified his lover. He spent the summer with his family in Ballylee, on the western Irish coast, before moving to Oxford, England.

Leda and the Swan was written in 1923 according to the given date; it is a depiction of a sexual encounter between a delicate young virgin and a strong, powerful, experienced older man. Yeats could have written it about himself and his wife, but in fact he did not write any sexual poetry about George.

Later in Among Schoolchildren Yeats said 'I dream of a Ledaean body' whilst grieving for his lover. In Nineteen Hundred and Nineteen he says:

Some moralist or mythological poet Compares the solitary soul to a swan; I am satisfied with that ...

So Leda and the swan represent Yeats and his lover.

Leda and the Swan

A sudden blow: the great wings beating still
Above the staggering girl, her thighs caressed
By the dark webs, her nape caught in his bill,
He holds her helpless breast upon his breast.

How can those terrified vague fingers push

The feathered glory from her loosening thighs,
And how can body, laid in that white rush,
But feel the strange heart beating where it lies?

A shudder in the loins engenders there
The broken wall, the burning roof and tower
And Agamemnon dead.
Being so caught up,
So mastered by the brute blood of the air,
Did she put on his knowledge with his power
Before the indifferent beak could let her drop?

Taking into account the intensity of emotion and the physical detail of the text, and that Yeats only writes about actual events and emotions in his life, he is talking about reality, not myth. It is not about his wife; they had no deep physical feelings for each other, despite their children. From 1919 his poetry is overtly physical and very amorous, but never merely affectionate except when it concerns George. Of course Yeats did not say publicly that he had a lover, because he was married. Similarly, when George later had an affair with Lennox Robinson, it was not made public. Acting as editor, George altered this poem's date of creation before it was published, and also delayed the date of publication. Furthermore Yeats never explained the context in which it was written to avoid the reactions of his wife, the public and religious people.

Despite living in Oxford, Yeats still needed to return to Dublin for his work and he did so alone. By 1919 he was writing Ego Dominus Tuus (Latin: I am your Master).

Hic. On the grey sand beside the shallow stream
Under your old wind-beaten tower, where still
A lamp burns on beside the open book

That Michael Robartes left, you walk in the moon
And though you have passed the best of life still trace,
Enthralled by the unconquerable delusion,
Magical shapes.

Ille.   By the help of an image
I call to my own opposite, summon all
That I have handled least, least looked upon.

Hic. And I would find myself and not an image.

Ille. That is our modern hope and by its light
We have lit upon the gentle, sensitive mind
And lost the old nonchalance of the hand;
Whether we have chosen chisel, pen or brush,
We are but critics, or but half create,
Timid, entangled, empty and abashed,
Lacking the countenance of our friends.

Hic.   And yet
The chief imagination of Christendom,
Dante Alighieri, so utterly found himself
That he has made that hollow face of his
More plain to the mind's eye than any face
But that of Christ.

Ille.   And did he find himself
Or was the hunger that had made it hollow
A hunger for the apple on the bough
Most out of reach? And is that spectral image
The man that Lapo and that Guido knew?
I think he fashioned from his opposite
An image that might have been a stony face
Staring upon a Bedouin's horse-hair roof
From doored and windowed cliff, or half upturned

Among the coarse grass and the camel-dung.
He set his chisel to the hardest stone.
Being mocked by Guido for his lecherous life,
Derided and deriding, driven out
To climb that stair and eat that bitter bread,
He found the unpersuadable justice, he found
The most exalted lady loved by a man.

Hic. Yet surely there are men who have made their art
Out of no tragic war, lovers of life,
Impulsive men that look for happiness
And sing when they have found it.

Ille.   No, not sing,
For those that love the world serve it in action,
Grow rich, popular and full of influence,
And should they paint or write, still it is action:
The struggle of the fly in marmelade.
The rhetorician would deceive his neighbours,
The sentimentalist himself, while art
Is but a vision of reality.
What portion of the world can the artist have
Who has awakened from the common dream
But dissipation and despair?

Hic.   And yet
No one denies to Keats love of the world;
Remember his deliberate happiness.

Ille. His art is happy, but who knows his mind?
I see a schoolboy when I think of him,
With face and nose pressed to a sweet-shop window,
For certainly he sank into his grave
His senses and his heart unsatisfied,
And made – being poor, ailing and ignorant,

Shut out from all the luxury of the world,
The coarse-bred son of a livery-stable keeper - Luxuriant song.

Hic.   Why should you leave the lamp
Burning alone beside an open book,
And trace these characters upon the sands?
A style is found by sedentary toil
And by the imitation of great masters.

Ille. Because I seek an image, not a book.
Those men that in their writings are most wise
Own nothing but their blind, stupefied hearts.
I call to the mysterious one who yet
Shall walk the wet sands by the edge of the stream
And look most like me, being indeed my double,
And prove of all imaginable things
The most unlike, being my anti-self,
And standing by these characters disclose
All that I seek; and whisper it as though
He were afraid the birds, who cry aloud
Their momentary cries before it is dawn,
Would carry it away to blasphemous men.

For the first time Yeats uses Latin, the common voice of Catholicism. Also for the first time he divides himself into two different personalities, Hic (Latin: me now) and Ille (Latin: him or the other one) Hic represents the public Yeats, the one with a position in the world, or 'Dante'[10] who is enthralled by 'the unconquerable delusion, Magical shapes', as befits a creator of moods and illusions, a mage, a playwright, a poet.

Ille on the other hand, also called Michael Robartes, is a shadow or ghost, a 'spectral image' who is at home with the straw beds and horses' excreta of Bedouin nomads or ordinary lower class people '... the coarse grass and the camel-dung'.

Ille says he has been 'mocked ... for his lecherous life' but has now found 'The most exalted lady loved by a man'. He has been playing the field for women, but now he has really fallen in love with the actual rather than the imagined one. He says 'I seek an image, not a book'; he is looking for beauty and flesh, not intellectual analysis as provided by his wife. The title of the poem tells us that his 'most exalted lady' is Catholic and their love has been consummated (I am your master), while the identity of the man as Ille implies that he is not talking about his wife. Ille has left an 'open book', a work still in progress.

In the last stanza Yeats asks his anti- self, the other version of himself called Michael Robartes, to

"disclose
All that I seek; and whisper it as though
He were afraid the birds ... would carry it away to blasphemous men."

In other words he is frightened of what will happen when 'the birds', or the public, know about his love. This tells us that he knows that society does not approve, though it is honest and innocent. He does not identify the 'blasphemous men' here, though he writes about them later as 'three old rascals'.

Yeats had been a poet all his life, rather like a modern pop musician or artist, creating his own works and presenting them by himself to his paying audience. He was financially dependent on his own efforts. It was to his advantage to be idolized, to create a following, a fan club. His influence in literary circles was broad, so that he was popular overseas as well as at home. He was celebrated everywhere for his ability to make people listen to him.

The politics of Ireland and the divisions within it appalled

Yeats, who craved unification of north and south, Catholics and Protestants, rich and poor, nationalists and unionists, as shown in his political slogan "Unity of Being'. Following the ideas of Augusta Gregory he believed that Irish divisions could be united by a shared culture: writing and story-telling, poetry and plays, music and dancing, singing and art.

When Yeats took his poetry to America in January 1920 he represented Ireland. He shared his venues with Eamon de Valera, who had recently escaped from Lincoln Jail in England for anti-British republicanism.[11] Therefore he was obliged to comment on political conflict in Ireland, such as the Boundary between Ulster and southern Ireland, the opposition of Protestant and Catholic faiths, and the fight for political independence and freedom from British control.

When Yeats carried out his two-week tour George accompanied him to New York. On arrival they met John Quinn at the Algonquin Hotel. Quinn had a new lover, and he made his new partner hide in a cupboard, ready to spring out and surprise the visitors when he signalled to her to do so. While hidden, she overheard them quarrelling. George was insisting that they must try for a son, as her menstrual timetable indicated, but her husband was very dismissive and said there was no need. Both were aware that Yeats had no need for sex with George. He later requested that George remain in New York with Quinn to visit his father, while he toured America alone. It is not known whether his lover accompanied him, since there is no record extant of any part of his tour. She was not shown on the passenger list, which included all those on board, on his ship to New York, though she may have caught a different one. Nor is there any record of her being in Dublin at that time.[12]

During his trip to America Yeats took part in an ouija board session and was surprised when his name appeared several times. "Yeats", said the script, "is a prince with an evil counsellor" and should "think of the principal of the double harness of Phaeton and the adverse principle."

Soon after his return to London another visionary left the following message: "The fight is still raging around you; whilst you are busy trying to increase the speed and usefulness of your chariot by means of a dark horse, you have parted with a winged white one which so long has served you faithfully and well. Unless you give the dark horse wings and subordinate it to the white horse, the latter will break away and leave you to the dark horse, who will lead your chariot into the enemies' camp where you will be made a prisoner. Conquer and subordinate the dark horse to the white one." In retrospect one can identify the 'evil counsellor' or 'dark horse' as George, and the 'white horse' as his lover.

Joseph Hone, Yeats's fellow senator, must have understood this, since he includes this tale in Yeats's biography. Yeats also found some truth in this for "a long time afterwards" and explained, "the warning had been both real and justified."[13]

Another 'message' was given to him by a local Abbé during a visit to Maud Gonne in Poitiers: "The voice said; 'He is to become an apostle; he must use his intelligence. If he does not, our Lord will take away his intelligence and leave him at the mercy of his heart.'" According to the Catholic Encyclopaedia, an apostle is someone sent forth and entrusted with a foreign mission; it means a delegate. Falling in love with a Catholic working class girl might well have been seen as an apostolic act for an Anglo-Irish senator in Free State Ireland.

A Sphinx with woman breast and lion paw

also known as
Bertha Georgie Hyde-Lees
Nemo Sciat
Nemo
George
The cat
All things known, all things unknown
The medium
The Instructor
Leo Africanus
The cage bird
The Frustrator
The Interpreter
Thomas
Ameritus
Dionertes
The witch
Mrs French
Woman won

Bertha Georgie Hyde-Lees was born in December 1892, but no one is sure of the exact date. According to her passport and birth certificate it was the 17th, but she and her mother, Nelly (Edith Ellen Hyde-Lees née Woodmass), always said it was the 16th, since the horoscopes for that day were better.[14] It is said to have happened at 8.25am, but she may have also chosen the time; there is no proof. Her given name was Bertha, but she seems always to have been known as Georgie.

Nelly, her mother, came from an aristocratic family, an "eccentric bunch" and had six siblings, but only she, the eldest, was legitimate; her mother was 'flirtatious and easily bored'. In 1887 Nelly had married Gilbert Hyde-Lees, captain of the 4th Battalion, Manchester Regiment. At that time he had two different addresses, but the couple soon moved to Brighton where Harold, their first child, was born in 1890. The following year they moved to Aldershot, where Bertha Georgie was born two years later.

Georgie's grandmother Mrs Woodmass "banished and disinherited" her daughter Nelly until 1927 for daring to talk openly about her mother's love affairs. However Nelly was just like her mother, 'flirtatious and easily bored' and had no time for her two children, who had lots of impressive godparents due to potential paternity. Some mysterious event happened to Georgie and Nelly on 29th November 1896, and another to Nelly on 27th December 1897, but no one knows any details except for the dates. The whole family was good at hiding embarrassing secrets. Moving house was a good way of avoiding embarrassing conflicts.

All this time there had been a nanny to look after the children, but in 1898 Harold was eight and started prep school as a boarder, so the nanny had to go. So from the age of six Georgie was educated at home.

In 1899 the Hyde-Lees had another new apartment at 17D de Vere Gardens, Kensington, where they enjoyed the good life of the better-off section of society. However a year later in 1900 Gilbert Hyde-Lees acquired a passport, and in 1901 he, Nelly and Georgie set off to Florence and rented accommodation on La Pietra, a hill outside the city. By March 1902 they had moved into Florence, but by July of the same year they were living at 38 Montpellier Street, Kensington. Shortly after they arrived there Georgie was sent to boarding school, aged ten. She had become a good reader, preferring to be alone, a watcher, very used to being tacit and keeping face in public because of her parents' problems.

As soon as she was in school the parents moved again to Carlisle Mansions, Westminster, and in 1905 to Yeomans Row nearby. Gilbert was in poor health as an inveterate alcoholic. Even Harold was affected at school by his parents' plight; he had become "a model of purity on the surface and a mine of dirt below, having learnt everything there was to know about evil from visits to Paris". Fairly soon after this, about 1907, Georgie's parents separated. Divorce was not possible except by passing a bill through parliament, which was very expensive and socially unacceptable. In any case, as Nelly had not ceased to be technically married, she could still rely on her husband's income. At any rate they were living apart: Nelly had moved to Kensington Palace Mansions, near de Vere Gardens, where she had first lived as a married woman, and Gilbert moved into separate accommodation.

Harold was now leaving school and preparing to go to Oxford, while Georgie, aged fifteen, was boarding at St James' School in West Malvern. She studied English, French, German, Latin and music as well as cookery, sewing, dancing and deportment. However she found it hard to fit in because she disliked being told what to do and hated bells and school timetables; after the chaos at home she could not settle to rigid routines. She left after only five terms. Instead she became a day pupil at a girls' school in London where she continued languages and added piano and singing, ballet and ballroom dancing, elocution, flower arranging and dressmaking. The school also arranged visits to theatre, opera and art exhibitions.

In 1909 Gilbert, now a patient at a home for alcoholics, died, the third generation of his family to die this way. Georgie was very sorry to lose her beloved father. Also later an alcoholic, she was currently over-controlled, hated being watched, hated routines, and she had already become expert at masking her inner fears with external joy and frivolity. Her biographer described her as "solitary", "cunning" and "wily". She had the facial flushing of an alcoholic, had nightmares and walked in her sleep. This had been exacerbated by frequent family rows and having to keep face in public despite desolate atmospheres at home, adulterous relatives, alcohol and constant changes of home and school. It all made Harold a wild teenager, and it made Georgie desperate for a stable home, physically and psychologically.

Nelly began to rebuild her social life by visiting salons and soirées to meet fashionable writers and poets, sometimes accompanied by Georgie. She was already acquainted with Olivia Shakespear, who was now editor of the 'Kensington', a new arts magazine featuring, inter alia, pieces by W. B. Yeats. As well as literature and poetry, Nelly, Olivia, her daughter Dorothy and Georgie shared a fashionable interest in the occult, horoscopes, Ouija boards and automatic writing.

Two years later, in 1911, Nelly married Harry Tucker, Olivia's brother. Olivia and Dorothy were their witnesses, but not nineteen-year-old Georgie. During the ensuing marriage Harry was occasionally violent towards his wife, but as he lent some stability and provided money nothing was made public. Meanwhile Georgie, now with enough money of her own, thanks to her father's death, enrolled at the Heatherley School of Art (where John Butler Yeats, William's father, had also studied). She stayed there almost a year with Dorothy, her new best friend. Georgie referred to herself as the "step-pest". Later for some unknown reason she destroyed her portfolio.

Five years before in 1906 Georgie aged 14 had been initiated into the Hermetic Order of the Golden Dawn. Her mother and

Dorothy were already members of this fashionable institution for the well heeled. It required avowed secrecy in all activities, along with constant self-scrutiny of conscience, motives, intentions and errors. William Butler Yeats initiated her, a famous, mature poet and senior mage. No wonder he fascinated her.

Georgie was an enthusiastic member of the Golden Dawn simply because men and women were treated as equals in whatever they did; no door was closed. The rites, costumes, chants and artifacts were exciting, spiritual and solemn, and their secret goals were for their own moral, educational and religious good. These objectives determined by the founder, Yeats, proved that he saw women as equal to men. In his lifetime there had been many changes in women's lives.[15] Yeats's occupations were nearly all gender-free: actors, poets, spiritualists and literary hosts could be either gender.

Eleven years later, in London in late September 1917, when Olivia formally introduced Yeats, her ex-lover, to her stepniece Georgie, she knew that he was looking for a young wife and hoped they would be compatible. From Olivia's point of view it would be very advantageous to be related to Yeats, and her niece would have a famous respected elderly husband who was expected to earn more during his lifetime. She might inherit from him and marry again when he died. If she had children, even one boy, she would be taken care of financially for the rest of her life.

Georgie was reasonably attractive, well off and well brought up with a cut-glass English accent. She shared Yeats' interests in literature, poetry and avant-garde writers, spoke three languages, could translate from Latin, and had learnt astrological rituals and how to read horoscopic charts in great detail. Her social manners were polished, and she had worked for the Red Cross. Ezra Pound had just become her brother-in-law, now that his affair with Iseult Gonne was over. There seemed to be no need for hesitation. Yeats and Georgie were married in haste, since there was no need to invite guests to Harrow Road Registry Office at 11.20am on 20th October 1917.

Yeats married Georgie because by then he needed a wife's income and an heir, not because he was desperate to marry her personally. He did it reluctantly, unwilling to give up his bachelor life as a free spirit, renowned poet and professional charmer. George married him because she idolised him. She was curious about sex; though not enamoured of children, she was capable doing what was necessary. Moreover she was already twenty-five, which counted as 'on the shelf', and she had few other marital prospects.

Like Georgie, Yeats had lived at many addresses as a youngster and his family had constantly moved on as a result of poverty, so he shared her craving for stability and putting a gloss over failures. He had developed masks to obscure his own feelings, either theatrical with the Abbey Theatre and poetry recitals, or astrological with the Golden Dawn. However he was used to expressing his feelings with honesty, though wise enough to see the world realistically. On the other hand George – after her marriage she made her name masculine – was not used to being honest about her father's alcoholism or her mother's and grandmother's affairs; she was more used to being tacit and hiding evidence.

The marriage was harmonious in most respects, but not sexually. They were not in love. George was an excellent housekeeper, astrologer and personal secretary, and was well liked at a certain distance by her new relatives. However on the honeymoon she cast an horary to ask " ... perche noi siamo infelice." (why we are unhappy). Within two years Yeats had started his affair with Lily; he must have assumed that George would understand if he took another lover, as this was her mother's and grandmother's tradition.

Marriage during their lives was associated with money, inheritance and allegiance rather than love, so it had long been accepted practice for both genders to have love affairs as long as they were kept relatively secret. Yeats himself had been having lucrative affairs with married women for at least twenty years and was well known as a Lothario; adultery had been much safer for his career than marriage or children, and had encouraged plentiful donations to his business ventures. His wife was also well acquainted with adulterous affairs; she herself was the product of one, since her mother was well known in that respect.

Immediately after their marriage George began having trances and producing 'automatic writing'. She told her husband that she was receiving messages from the other world and invented various names for her spirits. They were to be obeyed without question. This was done privately while Yeats was present, never otherwise. It was her way of gaining some control over her formidable husband. She gained control in other ways too. As a good hostess and administrator she quickly made herself invaluable at his Monday 'At Homes', chatting with his friends and colleagues, and serving food and drinks. She contributed towards his long poem 'The Vision', and many others too. "Mrs Yeats has continued to occupy a curious position ... it is generally known that her hand wrote many of [his] ideas..."[16]

George became further involved in her husband's professional life through the Abbey Theatre. Lennox Robinson had been manager since the end of 1909,[17] and she quickly built up a close relationship with him as she took over some of the backstage work, including costumes, make-up and scenery. After Yeats was chosen as a senator in 1923 she also befriended some of his colleague politicians, in particular Kevin O'Higgins, whom she described to her friend Lady Ottoline in Oxford as a 'coming' man. She invited him and his wife to dinner several times, so that he and Yeats knew each other well. In time she and O'Higgins grew very close indeed and spent a great deal of time talking together on their own.

O'Higgins was Catholic and nationalist, unlike Yeats, and, also unlike Yeats, he possessed a very forceful, determined personality. About 1916 he had become Captain of the Carlow Brigade of the Irish Volunteers (later the Irish Republican Army) and was imprisoned in 1918 for republicanism, after which he was elected Minister of Parliament for Queen's County (later Laois). After the first Dail was established in 1919 he was made Sinn Fein's Assistant Minister for Local Government, serving under W. T. Cosgrave, who thought him "not republican enough" because of his dismissal of the importance of the Irish language, and also of republican self-sufficiency, and his ardent engagement with militarism. When Cosgrave was arrested in 1920, O'Higgins suddenly became Sinn Fein's head of Local Government.

However in 1922 Sinn Fein split from the government, when the Free State Treaty was signed. As soon as this happened O'Higgins, without qualms of conscience, resigned from leading the Irish Republican Army, and became the new (British) Free State's Minister for Home Affairs. This showed that he was much more interested in power than in niceties of politics; very soon he stood for Leix-Offaly as Teachta Dála (T.D.), or Minister of Parliament.

As Home Affairs Minister at the outbreak of the ensuing civil war, O'Higgins feared that lengthy conflict would allow the British to reassert control, so with haste in the early part of 1923 he established a new Free State police force, the Garda Síochana. However General Richard Mulcahy, then Minister of Defence, commented during the following summer that "O'Higgins's personal presence in the Adjutant-General's office ... was ... of a person who didn't know what was going on."[18]

By September of that year indiscipline in the Garda was rife, so O'Higgins appointed Eoin O'Duffy as Commissioner. O'Duffy was a well-known Catholic nationalist who shared O'Higgins' fascist militarism. He had retired as head of the South Western Command of the Irish Republican Army after the civil war, so he knew how to organise well and win respect from his forces. Like O'Higgins he crossed over to the Free State because he was also more interested in power than politics.

But things were not going well for the Free State. In March 1924 an Army mutiny took place, and several important ministers resigned, including Mulcahy. Cosgrave also fell sick, leaving O'Higgins suddenly as the de facto head of government. Once in post, he immediately reversed Cosgrave's policy and decisively defeated the IRA who still wanted a republic. In June the same year he became Minister of Justice and External Affairs, all at once the strongest minister in government and blatantly fascist. In December he was also installed as Vice-President of the Executive Council of the Irish Free State, but retained his post as Minister of Justice.

He was now all-powerful in the fledgling state, and to prove it he ordered the execution of seventy-seven Republicans, fighters for a cause he had once espoused, as criminals. In protest, the Anti-Treaty Republican Army murdered his father and set fire to his family home in Laois. But this only made him more determined than ever to use fascist tactics.

O'Higgins recruited men who shared his fascist outlook, including David Neligan, who had once worked for the British administration at Dublin Castle. Whilst there, he had been one of Michael Collin's most important spies, supplying him with precise details about his victims' daily routines so that they could be individually and decisively attacked.

After Collin's demise in 1922, Neligan was promoted to Colonel in the IRA, but in 1923 he also changed allegiance and was made Chief Superintendent of Garda Síochana, with direct responsibility for 'G' Squad, the detective section. He was answerable directly to O'Duffy, who was answerable directly to O'Higgins. It was a chain of command through which any order could be instantly transmitted, yet secure enough to withstand any accusation. Accordingly Neligan's autobiography did not record anything after the civil war.[19]

By 1925 George Yeats was very friendly with O'Higgins. She had discovered someone as wily, cunning and cold-bloodedly efficient at finding solutions to problems as she was. They both saw themselves as better than others in terms of money, class, power and authority. Like many contemporary aristocrats in England, they were fascist supporters of Hitler, devoutly believing that certain types of people were 'unmenschlich' or 'non-human', so not worthy of attention. They both believed, like Hitler, that it was essential to accomplish their own goals regardless of the confines of law, religion or accepted morality, as their actions prove in retrospect.

George's problem could be presented as political: the power that young, rural, lower class, Catholic Lily O'Neill had over the mature, delicate, Anglo-Irish Protestant poet and Senator William Butler Yeats. Lily had become mother to Yeats's first-born son and heir, so she was in a position to blackmail him, whether she did or not. Yeats was even sharing his political ideas with her, they talked freely, as his poems revealed to his editor wife, and Lily could be seen as capable of passing top-secret information from him to her lower class friends in republican circles.[20]

Furthermore George understood that her stupid, reckless husband eventually wished to divorce her. After the birth of Lily's son he had uncharacteristically begun to show an interest in divorce legislation. She had talked to him at length about his properties and estate and about handing things down to the next generation – his poems were full of references to them[21] – but he still seemed set on marrying Lily.

O'Higgins was well known for using Michael Collin's technique via David Neligan: silent research on a specific enemy, before using fast, direct action to annihilate him. O'Higgins, or Neligan, had no trouble locating Lily because George supplied the necessary information. In his poem "A Prayer to My Son" Yeats talks of knowing the people who want to murder his son; they were O'Higgins and George, whom Yeats knew well. George was intelligent enough to be aware of her husband's fluctuating moods and preoccupations and watched him tacitly and closely. Her husband's trips to the club were regular, and he came back in a better mood. She was accustomed to her mother's adultery, so she followed him to where Lily lived. She also observed his expert change of appearance.

Yeats dressed up as Michael Robartes, a sexy younger working class man, to meet Lily. He would tell George he needed a quiet atmosphere in which to concentrate on his work, so he could be gone for days to the Hibernian Club[22] on St Stephen's Green in Dublin's centre, half way between his family home in Merrion Square and Lily's home in the Liberties. Only George and Yeats were capable of knowing where Lily was, Yeats because he went to see her secretly, George because only she could observe him disappearing and follow him.

Why would George have wanted to know where Lily lived? She was jealous of Lily and her son; moreover they threatened her social position and her own son's inheritance. These would be lost if he divorced and remarried. By 1925 she had been married to Yeats for seven years. By all accounts their wedded bliss had vanished after the birth of their daughter in 1919,[23] giving way to orders, with very little passion, from the "instructor' and various other voices emanating from George, about Yeats's behaviour and sexual functioning. She was not emotional, but she was very happy with their Georgian house and country castle representing stability. She was used to the prestige of being the wife of a mage, a poet, a politician. He was Anglo-Irish, Protestant and upper class in her mind, tall and relatively handsome, used to public speaking and an important member of government. How could she give all of that up?

Apart from losing her position and his possessions there was also the ignominy of becoming his rejected ex-wife, his discarded lover. How could Lily, this 'country wench', or 'green wing' be better than herself in any way? How could Yeats be in love with Lily and not with her?

George had been key to many aspects of Yeats' life, but her stars were fading. She had supplied him with money at the start of their marriage and was still a source of finance, although Yeats was now earning more. Recently he had been short of money due to expenditure on his new son and the mother, but George had not offered to help him, out of fear that her rival would benefit. George had been a member of the Golden Dawn long before they married and now belonged to Stella Matutina; however as a Senator he was now embarrassed by it. She had been part of the London literary world of salons and 'at homes', but he had now outgrown them. She had had his baby, but it was a girl. She redacted his poetry and articles before publication; he was grateful for the secretarial help, but not for her attempts to write with him. But despite all the failures, in the political world she was still his well-presented wife.

Meanwhile Lily was using her husband's money for the foster-mother and the baby, including rent, clothes and food, and their needs would grow in future. Yeats was growing poorer by the minute[24], so George's own lifestyle was being curtailed. In addition Lily's son was bound to usurp the Yeats inheritance if divorce took place. Therefore George felt desperate enough to find Lily and persuade her, by force if necessary, to renounce her claim on Yeats, and to go away.

There is no direct evidence about what subsequently happened, since George, O'Higgins and his officers systematically destroyed it, because their actions were illegal. To misquote Mandy Rice-Davies at the trial of John Profumo in 1963, "They would, wouldn't they?" However there is plenty of circumstantial evidence.

Firstly, Yeats wrote a poem about his fear of people he knew wanting to kill his son, and the son was obviously not

Michael. He knew a limited number of people closely, and spent most of his time with his wife, who naturally was very angry with his girlfriend and illegitimate son. Thus his wife and her close friends, including O'Higgins, were the obvious candidates.

Secondly, George befriended O'Higgins and, according to Saddlemyer, they became extremely close, much closer than Yeats was to O'Higgins or Mrs O'Higgins was to George. They were particularly close during 1925, according to various biographies, and often talked privately, so they had plenty of opportunity to pass secrets to one another.

Thirdly, only George knew when Yeats left the house for any period of time, and she was the only person he informed about his whereabouts, e.g. the Club. Therefore George was the only person who would know when he was probably going to meet Lily, and she was the only person who could follow him. She was also motivated to do so, as discussed previously.

Fourthly, she had access to all the places he normally went to. She was a member of every club he belonged to and she had complete access to the Abbey Theatre, especially to the wardrobe, since she often helped with make-up and costume. Thus she would be able to recognise Yeats in his working-class disguise, and, what is more, she would be able to disguise her own appearance.

Fifthly, because she followed Yeats she discovered only Lily's address, not Kevin's. Yeats had warned Lily, as shown in his poetry[25], about the threats from his wife and her friends, so that she had arranged for distance between herself, her son and his father. Kevin lived in a different location with a different name and identity.

George had given Lily's address to O'Higgins, who gave it to Neligan. Clandestinely surveying the house where Lily lived, Neligan discovered the undercover relationship between Lily's best friend, Madge Hopkins, and Dr Patrick Purcell, a married man. On examination of Peace Commissioner (magistrate) Dr Purcell's life, he noted the friendly relationship between the professional man and his local Garda Superintendent Leopold J. Dillon. They had worked together for the past year, building a congenial alliance in dealing with crime and disaster.

Supt. Dillon had joined the Garda as a Constable in 1923, but chose to leave the disorganised force after a few months. On rejoining the following year at his brother's request, when O'Duffy's and Neligan's arrival appeared to strengthen the force, he was immediately sent on a course and promoted to Superintendent of three large police districts south of Dublin, covering most of Wicklow and part of Carlow. Since he was only 25 years old by then he would have understood, even if it had not been made explicit, that he owed his boss a favour. Accordingly Dillon, who had been handed Lily's address and pseudonym by Neligan, was ordered to threaten her to have nothing more to do with Yeats.

The evening before he met with Lily, Dillon had visited a friend in Sandycove near Dublin, as stated later in his witness deposition, though it was never mentioned in court. O'Higgins lived in Sandycove. Dillon therefore seems to have had his orders directly from the Vice-President of the Executive Council of the Irish Free State and the Minister for Justice and External Affairs, and certainly felt that he would be protected regardless of what he did as long as he fulfilled his contract.

Supt Dillon therefore approached Purcell to ask him to drive his colleague to Dublin the next time he was meeting Bridie (i.e. Madge Hopkins), and to persuade her to bring her friend

Honor (i.e. Lily O'Neill) along too, as a blind date for Dillon. This was a foolproof way of setting up a meeting between Dillon and Honor Bright without raising her suspicions, since the date would innocently come from her best friend.

In 1925 the Irish Free State government was attempting to prevent the introduction of divorce bills "a vincula matrimonii" into the Dáil. As early as June 1924 Yeats was warning that this would affect the Boundary between Protestant Ulster and the Catholic Free State: if the Catholic south refused to conform to the Protestant north and to Britain, the current political and legal divide would yawn further apart. Yeats had introduced his political slogan 'Unity of Being', promoting a united Ireland, on becoming a Senator, when his illegitimate Catholic son was two years old. Now that he was aged four, he was not only trying to unify Catholics and Protestants, but also rich and poor.

The Divorce Bill was not part of Yeats' usual remit, Culture. All his functions to date in the Senate House, for example designing the Free State coinage and debating state education, had been related to his artistic talent or poetic creativity. His motive for involvement in this Bill therefore may have been to divorce his wife and marry his lover. From his poetry one can infer that his feelings for Lily were much stronger than those he felt for his wife. Thus in these unique circumstances he was prepared to stand up and oppose Cosgrave's government, whom he normally supported, who wanted the Bill defeated. Yeats wanted to pass the Divorce Bill for personal rather than political reasons.

The Bill was debated on 11th June 1925, which would have been Lily's twenty-fifth birthday, had she not been murdered two days before. It was also two days before Yeats's sixtieth birthday. The dates were personally very emotive, and he was still reeling in shock and despair. Speaking against such a controversial Bill was an unusual activity for him in any case, and for him its purpose had just evaporated. Some of his audience in the Senate House knew of his personal turmoil or were very curious about it. In retrospect, it is surprising in the circumstances that he stood up to speak at all.

However he had been told, either by his wife or by O'Higgins and his minions, that he had no choice but to preserve the appearance of order, and since the speech had been planned for months it must go ahead. There was stress and controversy with every word, from every angle. In his case divorce would have been contrary to the social norm because he had children and shared property. As a respected poet and stateman he was supposed to have greater integrity than most, but his life had included unorthodox occult activities frowned on by religious figures[26]. His affair was with an unsuitable person by current standards, and the fact that she had already given birth to his child added sparks to the fire.

Politicians who knew of his private life, such as Joseph Hone and Oliver St John Gogarty amongst others, recognised these facts, which accounts for the tense atmosphere and Yeats' passionate delivery. In particular it accounts for his last words: "... Genius has its virtue, and it is only a small blot on its escutcheon if it is sexually irregular."[27]

After Lily's death, George systematically edited or destroyed all of of Yeats's papers and his other belongings to rid them of any reference to Lily O'Neill or her son. Whether he knew or gave permission for it is a moot point, but they appear in retrospect to have been entirely his wife's actions, not his. Yeats appears to have relinquished control over George, who continued to keep an extraordinarily tight rein on his works after his death. She was well known for refusing permission to study certain texts, and for rebutting scholars who wished to explore certain conclusions.

And right between these two a girl at play…

Lily O'Neill, also known as
Mary Kate Neill
Catherine Neill
The Dancer
All things loved, all things unloved
Leda
Some green wing
Lizzie O'Neill
The country wench
The moon
The sailing moon
Helen
Homer's paragon
A peasant girl
The hare
Woman lost
A staring virgin
A living child
The Girl
That young child
The wild bird
Honor Bright
A woman young and old
The mermaid
The first of all the tribe
A proud woman

Other characters associated with her:

Madge Hopkins, also known as
Bridie
Peg or Meg

Margery

Margaret McGill, also known as
Madge
Old Madge
Peg or Meg
& James White
A woman and a man

Kevin Barry O'Neill, also known as
The Black Eagle
The Heir
The 4th daimon
Mummy wheat
...Some marvellous empty sea-shell flung
Out of the obscure dark of the rich streams, and not a fountain...
...The symbol which
Shadows the inherited glory of the rich.
The stone
The living stone
Kevin McGill
Barry Kevin O'Neill
The self-sown, self-begotten shape,
the grey-leaved olive-tree
/ Miracle-bred out of the living stone...
A shape...honey of generation had betrayed...
Chestnut tree, great-rooted blossomer...
The leaf, the blossom or the bole
Oedipus's son

Mary Kate Neill was born on June 11th 1900 in the tiny township of Graiguenaspiddoge in County Carlow. The 1901 census shows her ten months old. Her mother was Catherine or Kate Neill, née Cullen, aged 38, and her father Michael Neill aged 51. He was a blacksmith, born just after the potato famine of 1845-7. Graiguenaspiddoge was a row of 28 houses beside a main road in the countryside, and the family lived in house 23 according to the censor, though the houses were not numbered. Mary Kate had three older brothers and two older sisters. Because her mother was Kate and her sister Mary she was always called Lily. Edward was the eldest; his birth certificate in 1885 names his father as Patrick Neill, who died early. Kate's next son, whose father was Michael Neill, was named Patrick after him. In marrying Kate, Michael had assumed responsibility for his brother's widow and child.

The 1911 census shows Graiguenaspiddoge smaller, with only 25 houses. The Neill family has now moved to house 14, halfway down the street. Edward is no longer listed because he left for America in 1905 aged 20, according to Ellis Island records. His stepfather had died in Staplestown Road, Carlow, aged 53 in 1903. Mary, registering his death, identified him as a mason. Their mother, a 'blacksmith's widow' died in 1908 aged 46 of 'gastritis' and 'exhaustion'.

The remaining orphaned siblings lived with Patrick Neill, 20, as head of the family. Julia, now 15, was living a few doors away as a servant. Mary, Michael and 11-year-old Lily, now officially called Catherine, were still at home. There was also another resident, a 22-year-old 'sister' called 'Julia Neill' according to the census; she seems to have been Patrick's partner because he later moved to America with her. Patrick and Michael were listed as labourers. No occupation was required for 'Julia' or Mary as they were women, and Catherine was a 'scholar'. All could read and write, were single and Roman Catholic.

All were adult except Lily. There was no work for the unqualified, locally or throughout Ireland, and no hope of further education or training without paying. Irish people were despised by the British: in front of most lodging houses on the mainland was a brass plaque bearing the words "No Blacks, No Irish, No Dogs". Irish people were rarely eligible for white-collar work, being viewed as ignorant or mad.[28] Their best option therefore was to save enough money to emigrate to America or Australia, or work the passage on a ship. They already had a sponsor in America, their brother Edward. Patrick and the older 'Julia' emigrated first, followed by Mary employed as a seamstress. Michael stayed at home and by 1930 he was married. He and his son were both called 'Mick the tip' because of the metal tips they wore on the toes of their shoes.[29] What happened to their sister Julia is unknown. It is probable that none of them ever knew their younger sister as Honor Bright.

By 1917 most of Lily's relatives had vanished from her life through death or emigration. The emigrants had paid their own passage, so she was expected to work as hard as they had done, saving her money to follow them as soon as possible. According to Yeats's poetry she wanted to go to college; that might be possible in America, but not in Ireland for a poor Catholic girl. Therefore in 1918 she found a job in Dublin as sales-assistant-cum-model at a respectable ladies outfitter[30] near Trinity College. It included tied lodgings and clothes, meaning low wages; she had to earn more for the ship to America. She was young and attractive, therefore happy to be employed as a dancer in an evening club. Her customers paid for one dance at a time but she took no notice of them; she "outdanced thought".

Yeats was used to assessing young women as actresses or stagehands, at literary soirées or occult meetings. One can imagine him, only ten minutes' distance on foot from the United Arts Club in his alter ego as Michael Robartes, watching her and being desperately impressed by her earnest, naïve beauty. He had spent the last few years looking for a fertile woman to be his wife; how could he ignore her virtues?

On a Picture of a Black Centaur by Edmund Dulac, written September 1920 according to the given date, reinforces this, as Yeats clearly describes his affair:

Your hooves have stamped at the black margins of the wood,
Even where horrible green parrots call and swing.
My works are all stamped down in the sultry mud.
I knew that horse-play, knew it for a murderous thing.
What wholesome sun has ripened is wholesome food to eat,
And that alone; yet I, being driven half insane
Because of some green wing, gathered old mummy wheat
In the mad, abstract dark and ground it grain by grain
And after baked it slowly in an oven; but now
I bring full-flavoured wine out of a barrel found
Where seven Ephesian topers slept and never knew
When Alexander's empire passed, they slept so sound.
Stretch out your limbs and sleep a long Saturnian sleep;
I have loved you better than my soul for all my words,
And there is none so fit to keep a watch and keep
Unwearied eyes upon those horrible green birds.

A centaur is a symbol of wanton male sexuality. Its blackness denotes covert or immoral events such as adultery, outside the light. Yeats says in the poem "Your hooves have stamped at the black margins of the wood" which means he has been active outside his area, in other words where the anti-treaty IRA and committed nationalists meet, and where his poetry is treated with contempt and 'stamped down".

The "horrible green parrots" are Irish nationalists whose colour is green, and who were then parroting political demands. Thus when he says he is "...being driven half insane / Because of some green wing..." he is referring to his lover from that section of society. Lily was well acquainted with "those horrible green birds". He admits "I knew that horse-play..." meaning sex outside marriage, though he knows he ought to have stayed with "...what wholesome sun has ripened..." or his wife, George. He "knew it for a murderous thing", so he is aware of murder as a result of adultery. He may have associated murder with George, but his meaning is not clear.

Nevertheless he has "gathered old mummy wheat ...". Wheat from the tombs of Egyptian mummies had recently been discovered to sprout centuries later, when removed from the dark and brought into the light. Yeats is talking about his potency; his seeds have sprung to life after having been dead for an age. "...In the mad, abstract dark... " refers to night, when sex happens, but also to the illicit nature of it. "Mummy wheat" refers to pregnancies of Lily and George in 1919, 1920 and 1921, subsequently exposed to the sun that has "...baked [them]..." and turned them into the "...full-flavoured wine..." of new children.

He says "I have loved you better than my soul for all my words..." This love has been detrimental to his soul, or morality and conscience. For this reason, and because of its exultant, joyful intensity, it is not written for George. The given date of the poem, September 1920, was just before the birth of his and Lily's illegitimate son.

The final two lines show why Yeats first got to know Lily. He trusted her knowledge of 'those horrible green birds', Sinn Fein or nationalist anti-treaty supporters, most of whom were Catholic. Having grown up in Carlow, she was automatically part of that society, just as he was part of the Anglo-Irish ruling class. However she was no political activist; she belonged to no group[31] and was more interested in emigration. However George would have interpreted these lines to mean that Lily was his spy, and that Lily might use him as her spy.

The previous year George had given birth to a daughter and had been angry at not having a son. George "never knew /When Alexander's empire passed": the new son she had been hoping for had been born to her husband's 'green wing'.
Yeats called Kevin his 'heir', his 'black eagle' or '4th daimon'. These phrases were found on a note written by Yeats shortly after Kevin was born in November 1920. To obscure their meaning, George claimed to have had a vision of an eagle, as though she had foreseen the birth of her own son the following August, although Michael had not yet been conceived.

In The Double Vision of Michael Robartes, also written in 1920, Yeats talks of this triangle as

'A Sphinx with woman breast and lion paw,
A Buddha, hand at rest,
Hand lifted up that blest;
And right between these two a girl at play...

He explains

'a girl my unremembering nights hold fast', in other words that he was sleeping with her, and feeling
'a crazy juice that makes the pulses beat', so that he is

... caught between the pull
Of the dark moon and the full...,,

between his wife and his lover. Yeats sees himself as Buddha, a benign public figure, a deified man blessing the multitudes. In contrast George is the Sphinx, a clairvoyant sculpted from cold, hard stone talking in riddles. She had "a woman breast" because had had his child, but she was simultaneously a wild, unrestrained predator inflicting terror with her overpowering 'lion paw'.

Yeats continued to meet Lily from 1919 until 1925. During some of this time they were far apart, such as when Yeats and George were living in Oxford. Before moving there, Yeats usually met Lily in her room, or else at his house, 73 St Stephen's Green, let to Maud Gonne. Yeats described in detail in his own poetry (quite separate from what he wrote with George) how he and Lily met, fell in love, where they met and his joy at having a son.[32]

Mrs Margaret McGill, a widow in her late forties with no children,

"...barren as a breaking wave...,"

was known for having nursing skills. She lived in the cellar at 2, Catherine Street, the Coombe[33] with her partner James White and his son. This was one of the poorest parts of Dublin in the early 1920s.

Yeats, or else his friend Dr Oliver St John Gogarty, a surgeon who was a volunteer at the Coombe Lying-In Hospital[34], had placed Lily in a room above Mrs McGill during the final months of her pregnancy. Mrs McGill looked after her before and after the baby was born. It was thanks to her skills as midwife and foster-mother that mother and child flourished.

When she moved into 2 Catherine Street, Lily changed her name to Lizzie O'Neill and this was the name that appeared on her son's birth certificate. This was almost certainly done at Yeats's insistence; he had already referred in '...A Picture of a Black Centaur' to his adultery being 'a murderous thing'. He had previously attempted to end his association with Lily by moving with his wife to Oxford; now that he was back in Dublin and under obligation to his lover and her son – he was paying for their medical care, foster mother, accommodation, food and clothing – he was very fearful of someone's 'murderous' reaction. This must have been his wife's, since no other person would have known of his lover and son at this time apart from Maud, Gogarty and Dr Bethel Solomons, the gynaecologist.

Lily gave birth to Kevin Barry[35] on 9th November 1920 at the Coombe Lying-In Hospital. No father was named on the birth certificate, so her son took her own surname, O'Neill. The expected date of delivery was 40 weeks after conception according to current medical reckoning, however first-born children usually emerge about ten days after the projected date. Kevin was conceived on the weekend of 10th-11th January 1920[36], and was born two weeks after the estimated time of delivery.[37]

That weekend Yeats was in Liverpool viewing his ship for New York, SS Carmania, while George was in London working on William Blake at the British Library. Lily may have spent the weekend with him in Liverpool, or he may have taken the ferry to Dublin to stay overnight. Two days later on 13th January Yeats embarked with George on his promotional tour of America. John Quinn, his agent in New York, certainly knew about Lily. Yeats and his wife arrived back in Oxford on the 7th June 1920.

Halfway through July Yeats suddenly received a letter from Maud, writing from his house in Dublin where she was still living. There was desperate urgency about Iseult's marriage to Francis Stuart. Stuart, nine years younger than his wife Iseult and still only eighteen, had

"...beaten her, burned her clothes, sold her engagement ring, but managed to get her pregnant nonetheless."[38]

A few hours later Maud sent another urgent letter telling Yeats

"...he need not bother to come to Ireland, although she would be grateful for a chance to talk to him about Iseult's condition. (Except to George, don't mention to anyone that I think there is a child on the way.)"

Yeats arrived nevertheless in Dublin the very next day, alone. George later reported to her biographers that she had to stay in Oxford as she was expecting his sister Lily to visit, and she thought she might be pregnant. Maud's letters are extant, but whether other sheets accompanied them is not known.

This explanation poses several questions. Maud had been renting Yeats's Dublin house at 73 St Stephen's Green for the last few months and she had regularly corresponded with her own daughter about this undesirable marriage. So what exactly had occasioned the sudden urgency of this letter? All the information we have emanates from George, who as editor of Yeats's letters may have suppressed something.

Maud was by now a Sinn Fein republican judge in the Free State, and was well known for running nationalist homes and classes for Irishwomen in Dublin, so she already had all of the contacts she needed to cope with problems in Iseult's marriage. She did not need to call on Yeats who was unqualified and living in a different country. In any case he had not seen Iseult for three years since he married. Before that she had had a turbulent affair with Ezra Pound in London, turned down Yeats's proposal of marriage in 1917, and now he did not get on with her new teenage radical republican husband at all.

Even though Maud had told him explicitly in her second letter that he was not needed, he still travelled to Dublin with great speed and felt "…invigorated, even euphoric, wafted by the smell of violets…"[39] as he checked into St Stephen's Green Hibernian Club. No explanation was given for his euphoria. From here we are told he travelled to Glenmalure to see Iseult and interviewed witnesses about the behaviour of Stuart. Then according to George, for it is her account that Maddox is relating, he consulted Bethel Solomons, "Dublin's leading gynaecologist". Shortly thereafter Iseult, who was heavily pregnant, was admitted to hospital in Glenmalure with restraints on Stuart visiting. There is however no evidence to show whether Yeats was involved with the hospital, or what involvement a gynaecologist in Dublin who had not examined Iseult could possibly have.

After her husband had been gone for some weeks, George sent him a letter to say she had just had a miscarriage. Yeats informed Dr Solomons, but his wife stayed in Oxford and Yeats did not go home. Maddox says they sent 'effusive and loving" letters to each other, "George … vowed to meet him in London so that they could have dinner together without Lily around."[40] It is not clear to which 'Lily' George was referring. Yeats's sister Lily was with George in Oxford at this time; however she had not been aware of any miscarriage.[41] George had invented her own pregnancy and miscarriage to make her husband downgrade his lover's pregnancy. She was being jealous, manipulative and dishonest.

Yeats told George that Iseult was rationed to six cigarettes a day and was being examined by a "lunacy doctor". This was odd because according to Maud, Stuart was mad, not Iseult. However such treatment would have been appropriate for an anxious, starving, unmarried mother who had been living rough for around two months, such as Lily O'Neill. If Iseult had been starved, as claimed, by her husband, her photographs never showed it; she always appears very well fed. If the medical treatment did refer to Lily, then Yeats was telling George about Lily's state of health, not Iseult's; he was keeping his wife up to date with developments in his lover's condition.

By late July, when Yeats received Maud's letter, Lily was approximately twenty-seven weeks pregnant, i.e. six months. After hiding her pregnancy from employers for approximately four months, on discovery she would have been sacked on the spot and viewed as disgusting and immoral. When she lost her job she had lost friends as well as income, lodgings, food, clothing and medical care. For six to eight weeks she had been living rough as a 'fallen woman'.[42]

As she had previously met Yeats in Dublin, she knew the address of his house; and since Maud, a Catholic Sinn Fein judge and well-known women's social worker, was renting it she approached Maud for help. Maud then contacted Yeats in confidence using Iseult as an excuse, since she was also pregnant and experiencing marital difficulties. This accounts for the urgency and confidentiality of her letter, and is a far more plausible explanation of why Yeats felt it so important to ignore her advice and travel to Dublin without delay. It also explains why he contacted the gynaecologist so quickly; Maud had no problems in arranging for her daughter to see medical personnel when she thought fit, so he was doing this for his own interests. Nevertheless when George claimed that she was pregnant and to have had a miscarriage, he did not contact a gynaecologist or any other doctor. Yeats obviously did not believe her, so did not react.

This confused story of Maud's letter and its consequences is based solely on George's account of what happened. Yeats never said or wrote anything about this episode, apart from his euphoric reaction on arriving in Dublin.

The following October Lily was expected to give birth, and Yeats suddenly decided to have his tonsils out in Dublin, with Gogarty operating. George tells us that first of all Yeats went to consult a nameless doctor in Harley Street

"even though George wanted him to have the operation in Dublin. When he got to London, he found he had the wrong address but then could not find the correct one in the telephone book. Going back to Oxford defeated, Yeats realised that he had not found the surgeon's double-barrelled name because he had looked it up under the second half. George consulted the stars about Yeats's 'mistake'.

'They said,' Yeats reported to Quinn, 'quite plainly that if I went to the London operator I would die, probably of hemorrhage.[43] On the other hand, the omens for Dublin were 'as favourable as possible – Venus, with all her ribbons floating, poised upon the mid-heaven! Off he went to Dublin where Gogarty took out the offending tonsils with great aplomb and pronounced next day, looking into the poet's throat, 'I have been too thorough.' "[44]

Yeats had been told in the USA earlier that year that he needed a tonsilectomy, but had put it off as unnecessary. Neither Yeats nor George had recorded any problems with his throat in the weeks or months since their return. Now that the tonsillectomy was suddenly urgent, the question of whether

Yeats should go to Harley Street, London or to Dublin for the operation was strange, because he lived in Oxford where a local doctor or hospital could have treated him, or a private one if he so desired. Why did he need to travel at all? Harley Street would cost at least double the rate. But Yeats's health was rarely mentioned; so why on earth was it necessary to give a detailed story of this event?

George Yeats supplied the version that Maddox writes, whereas the quotes are from Yeats writing to John Quinn. Assuming once again that George had manipulated the truth, the most likely scenario is that Yeats had said that he needed the operation and that his friend Gogarty would do it in Dublin, but George preferred that he should have it done in London, away from Lily. To prove her point she had consulted the stars, as she usually did for greater authority, but the stars let her down by showing that his suggestion was better.

Yeats therefore had his operation carried out in Dublin at short notice by his friend Gogarty, an eminent ear, nose and throat surgeon. It was a very simple operation; most tonsillectomies were carried out at home on kitchen tables until the 1950s, and full recovery took only a week. Nevertheless Gogarty said the following day that he had been 'too thorough', that he had messed up this simple procedure, thereby giving Yeats an excuse to stay in Dublin for a month.

Yeats knew of his wife's seething anger at his adultery; Lily and her son had been threatened with murder. He was seriously frightened and had warned her to protect herself from "the yelling pack" that he describes in the fourth poem of "A Man Young and Old", called"The Death of the Hare". The hare, Lily, is vulnerable; the pack of hunting dogs is running after her. He says he had alerted the hare to the pack and to the safety of the wood – to become another tree in the forest or change her identity for anonymity - but he remembers "her distracted air". She did change her name, but she kept her surname, the tenth most common in Ireland. On Kevin's birth certificate his mother is Lizzie O'Neill.

In 1922 Yeats moved back to Dublin from Oxford because the civil war had ended after the signing of the Treaty. The Irish Free State had been declared with much controversy, but Yeats supported it, was respected by the British government and also by the Anglo-Irish ruling class and so was offered a position in the new Irish government as a unionist senator. As it was paid work he was very happy to accept it. According to Brenda Maddox's biography of Yeats he was always short of money around this time.

At the same time as the Yeats family moved back to Dublin, Lily adopted a new name probably suggested by Yeats: Honor Bright depicts an honorable, bright, young woman. Also at the same time, now that Kevin was weaned, she moved away from the rented room above Kevin to a single room on the first floor of 48 Newmarket.[45] Her new address was situated next to a busy police station; newspapers that subsequently insinuated that it was a brothel were ridiculously wide of the mark.

Madge Hopkins suggested this house containing only single women because it was her own address. Madge knew her friend as Lizzie, so they had met during Lily's late pregnancy or childbirth, in the hospital; therefore Madge had also been an unmarried mother. Lily was moving to Newmarket in order to keep her son's address and identity secret, but Madge had no child to look after.

Pregnant unmarried girls were always sacked from work and were usually thrown out by their families as soon as the pregnancy became obvious. When homeless, they were admitted for board and lodging in the local workhouse or occasionally in a convent, on condition they worked every day. Lily was not registered at any such institution in Dublin.

Food, clothing and accommodation for two, plus time off work to feed the baby, were unattainable luxuries for a workhouse inmate, and "loose woman" or "fallen angel" were vicious labels applied to unmarried mothers. So after birth the baby was inevitably given up to a children's home for adoption.

But Lily had kept her son; he had one-to-one care from a dedicated foster-mother and she had lived above them. This indicated that all her bills were paid. In Dublin in the 1920s only children from wealthier families were cared for full-time by a foster-mother. From the time that Lily was sacked from her job in 1920 until the time of her murder in 1925 she had financial help to pay for food, clothing and the foster-mother. When Gogarty eagerly phoned Yeats in 1922 to tell him that he had won the Nobel Prize for Literature, he was shocked that his friend's first reaction was to ask how much it was worth.

As revealed by his poetry, Yeats had split his appearance into two masks (or more) by 1918, William Butler Yeats and Michael Robartes. After 1919 he split his whole personality into two separate individuals, a widely respected, elderly upper class Senator, poet and theatre manager, and a younger working class man with a Catholic lover and a son. This was a completely new interpretation of 'Unity of Being', his political slogan of 1918 to 1925, during his involvement with Lily.

In "A Prayer For My Son" Yeats writes:

Bid a strong ghost stand at the head

That my Michael may sleep sound,
Nor cry, nor turn in the bed
Till his morning meal come round;
And may departing twilight keep
All dread afar till morning's back,
That his mother may not lack
Her fill of sleep.

Bid the ghost have sword in fist;
Some there are, for I avow
Such devilish things exist,
Who have planned his murder, for they know
Of some most haughty deed or thought
That waits upon his future days,
And would through hatred of the bays
Bring that to nought.

Though You can fashion everything
From nothing every day, and teach
The morning stars to sing,
You have lacked articulate speech
To tell Your simplest want, and known,
Wailing upon a woman's knee,
All of that worst ignominy
Of flesh and bone;

And when through all the town they ran
The servants of Your enemy,
A woman and a man,
Unless the Holy Writings lie,
Hurried through the smooth and rough
And through the fertile and waste,
Protecting, till the danger past,
With human love.

In the second line Yeats names his son as Michael, the son of George born on 22nd August 1921. The given date of this poem is December 1921, four months after his birth. However the poem does not appear to be focussed on Michael, for in 1920-21, when the civil war in Ireland was in full swing, the Yeats family was living in peace in England. They had been in Oxford since 1919, after George had discovered her husband's lover. Just as her father had done on discovering her mother's affairs, George had moved her own family away as soon as she found out.

Yeats talks of knowing someone who is jealous; only George would know of and be jealous of his beloved first son by Lily, and Yeats would be the only person to hear about her jealousy, since knowledge of adultery and illegitimacy was kept well away from the public. Yeats says "Some there are ...", so he knows of danger to Lily and Kevin from at least two people.

The "most haughty deed or thought" was prior birth, since Kevin had been born ten months before Michael. As first-born son Kevin could become first in line to inherit from his father if Yeats wished[46]. George was threatening to kill Lily in order to protect her own children's inheritance, and had spoken to Yeats extensively about this in private. Yeats' anxiety about his property is present in "Meditations in Time of Civil War", written in 1921, according to the given date.

".... Out of life's own self-delight had sprung
the abounding glittering jet; though now it seems
As if some marvellous empty sea-shell flung
Out of the obscure dark of the rich streams,
And not a fountain, were the symbol which
Shadows the inherited glory of the rich.

The title of this poem sets it "... in time of Civil War", referring only to the time in which it was written, not to the content of the poem which talks of legal claims of inheritance to his property, rather than violence by marauders. The two sections are entitled "Ancestral Houses" and "My House", while the "fountain" represents his legitimate offspring, and the "empty sea-shell flung out of the obscure dark of the rich streams" is an accident, an illegitimate child. Yeats is contemplating which son, illegitimate or legitimate, should inherit his wealth.

In the last verse Yeats compares the civil war in Dublin and necessary protection of his infant son, to the Biblical story of Mary and Joseph journeying to Nazareth:

"... when through all the town there ran / The servants of Your enemy..."

Both Herod's soldiers in Jerusalem and O'Higgins National Guard in Dublin were on a mission to kill one particular infant boy.

Had Yeats and George actually been in Dublin, and had they felt personally threatened by the violence and disorder of that place and time, this poem might have referred to Michael. But although Yeats no doubt followed news of events in Ireland's capital very closely, he and his family were not involved in the war at all. Avoidance of the unrest of the Irish civil war was at least part of the reason they lived in England at that time.

On the other hand Kevin was actually born in Dublin one year earlier in November 1920 during the Civil War, and was actually threatened by random acts of violence because he lived so near to the city centre. Moreover he was definitely under threat from George Yeats who was appalled that her husband's possessions should now go to his eldest son rather than to her own son.

Kevin's foster-parents, Margaret McGill and James White, were raising him alongside a "brother" amid the daily chaos in Dublin; they were the "woman and the man."

Yeats' sons' names, Kevin and Michael, each have two syllables with stress on the first, so that one name could easily be substituted for another. In fact "Kevin' elides more easily than "Michael' in the second line of the first stanza.

In later life Michael said that whilst at school he was intensely embarrassed by the poem, which he did not understand at all. George edited her husband's works, so no one but she can have changed the dates and names before publication.

When dealing with the civil war Yeats has no antagonism towards either army. In "The Road at my Door" he does not differentiate between the Irregular and the Lieutenant, one from the IRA and the other from the Black and Tans. In "The Stare's Nest by my Window" he says there is
"More substance in our enmities
Than in our love".

It is all "senseless tumult" to him, ruled by "brazen hawks". He is very glad to "turn away and shut the door". It is the passion involved that entrances him, the determination to fight for what you believe in. He says in "The Road at my Door" that he feels "envy", of having a definite stance, of being sure enough to fight. He is much more focussed on his quandary over Kevin than on the civil war.

The Three Old Rascals

In 1922 Gogarty had nominated Yeats to be senator in the new Irish Free State. In 1923 he was awarded the Nobel Prize for Literature. By then he was renowned as a thoughtful, honest, imaginative man who was trustworthy, reliable, impartial and concerned for the whole of society.

In 1926 policemen had to be male, physically fit, of imposing build, able to handle a gun, and able to gain control of the local populace by force if necessary; Leopold J. Dillon fitted the picture exactly. Born in Cardiff in 1900, he was the same age as Lily O'Neill. However she came from a dirt-poor rural Irish family, whereas he was brought up in Wales and was relatively affluent. Tall, strong and formidable, he was said to have enlisted in the British Army and become Second Lieutenant by 1917, when he was discharged. However there is no evidence of this.

Evidence does show that he enlisted as a Private in the Artists Rifles in 1919, Regimental number 8752. It was an officer training corps whose recruits had to be recommended for entry, so he would have expected to become Second Lieutenant. However the corps was taken off live duty in 1920 and became a part-time territorial force, so he was demobbed before he reached promotion.

On discharge he enrolled as a medical student at Trinity College, Dublin and studied for one year, but did not qualify for the second.

On 20th August 1923 he joined the newly established Garda Siochana as a Constable, but resigned from this undisciplined force on 12th November the same year.[47] Subsequently however, when Eoin O'Duffy had become the new Commissioner and Sinn Fein's Colonel David Neligan had become head of 'G' Force, the detective force, his brother persuaded him to rejoin; he did so on 10th December 1924. After a six-week course he was promoted on 6th February 1925 to the post of Superintendent of three large police districts south of Dublin, covering most of Wicklow, part of Carlow and half of Kildare. He was only 24 years old, but his military officer training, health, imposing appearance and also the severe shortage of men after the First World War would have influenced this decision.

Based in the small town of Dunlavin, Dillon's most southern district included Blessington. As well as being a full-time, inexperienced Superintendent, Dillon was known to have at least one other part-time occupation, working as a 'screw' or warder at Mountjoy Prison in Dublin.[48] His Army experience, including military techniques and use of ammunition, were useful for various short contracts, and his physical presence gave him great authority.

In 1925 Patrick Purcell was married and of average height. He had done his medical training at Trinity College in Dublin and become General Practitioner at Blessington, a prosperous town in County Wicklow. Married with two children, he had also become the local Peace Commissioner, acting as magistrate and carrying out medical duties for the local constabulary. He worked closely with Superintendent Dillon to prevent and punish crime. He was only thirty, but police were very much depleted in personnel as a result of the First World War; so many men had been killed or badly injured. That meant there were also many lonely young women, therefore, like so many other married men, he had a clandestine lover in Dublin called Bridie whom he met two or three times a month. Her real name was Madge Hopkins; she was Lily's best friend.

Dillon approached Purcell on the afternoon of Tuesday June 8th 1925 at a summer fête in Blessington and asked for use of his sports car, as his own motorbike was out of commission. It was the hottest day of the year, and he asked Purcell to drive him to Dublin for a meeting,[49] since Purcell would be meeting Bridie that evening. Dillon also suggested Bridie should bring along her friend as a blind date for himseelf.

At 7.30 in the morning of Wednesday June 9th 1925, a hot sunny morning, Felix Reilly was walking past Ticknock crossroads outside Dublin to fetch his horses for the day's work. He saw a young woman lying on the ground and went to wake her, thinking she was asleep. Then he noticed some blood on her chest; she was dead. He ran a quarter of a mile to the only house in this rural location, a pub called Lamb Doyle's, and the eponymous landlord phoned the police.[50]

Superintendent John Reynolds arrived soon after, accompanied by a police sergeant with a camera. His photographs showed the location of the body, the ground around it and the wound.[51] Reynolds also informed the Coroner, Dr J.P. Brennan, who arrived about an hour later. He had served under Michael Collins and was an experienced judge and magistrate, well respected for his honesty.[52] After examining the body and wound in situ they removed it to the outhouse of the nearby public house. By this time a crowd had gathered and there was soon a queue to see the body.[53]

Despite the recent civil war and the long-standing political unrest, this murder was completely shocking to the general public, who flocked to hear and read everything available about it. Crowds gathered to hear Brennan's inquest. Interest was so high that every newspaper, broadsheet or tabloid, national or local, secular or religious, unionist or republican, in English or Irish language had front-page headline articles on it for weeks.⁵⁴

Coroner Brennan opened the inquest the following morning by deprecating the local population because they were unwilling to volunteer to be on the jury despite enormous popular interest, or perhaps because of it; Yeats' affair with Honor Bright was already fairly well known within parts of Dublin where everyone knew each other. Brennan made a short speech about the victim, a young lady about 26. Her clothes were undisturbed and the bullet had killed her instantly; in his estimation she was "a decent, innocent victim of a heinous crime", and he hoped the perpetrator would soon be caught and punished.⁵⁵

At about 2pm on Thursday 10th June, while the inquest was still in progress, Commissioner Eoin O'Duffy appeared without warning. He took Brennan aside, told him to adjourn the inquest for three weeks, and informed him that he would be taking over the case himself and relieving Brennan and Reynolds of their responsibilty for it. Both were to relinquish their posts for this case. Both had been seasoned British professionals long before southern Ireland became a Free State, so both objected to this absurd change to the normal routine. Their views were never heard in public, but Superintendent Reynolds was very angry.⁵⁶

Brennan adjourned the inquest and left the body in the pub outhouse so that relatives could come forward and claim the body for burial, but no relatives had appeared by the next day. The police authorities subsequently buried the corpse at Kilgobbin cemetery near Stepaside after the second post-mortem ordered by Neligan had taken place, approximately on 1st July, well before a judge could check its controversial findings.

Also on Wednesday the 10th June, Supt. Dillon gave himself up and admitted to the murder. Two days later his accomplice, Dr Purcell, was arrested. Chief Supt. Col. David Neligan had them both in custody in Dublin Castle by the 12th June.

Three weeks later O'Duffy allowed Neligan to resume the inquest at a local school. Public feeling was higher and had not dissipated at all. Once again loud, incredulous throngs of people gathered. Rumours were rife about what had been done and why.

The Garda were under pressure. The new Free State was anxious to establish its political credentials to the rest of the world, to show that it could function well without British influence; if it could not, Britain would re-establish control. It was extremely important therefore to play down the fact that individuals from the Garda Siochana had carried out this murder, and to absolve Free State politicians of acting outside the law. They had to prevent the public, who doubted their integrity, from insurrection, and reassert political authority.

David Neligan was already a famous figure. He had worked for Michael Collins, the great Irish Nationalist who signed the Anglo-Irish Treaty in December 1921, creating the Irish Free State, a self-governing British colony similar to Canada. Collins had previously worked as a British civil servant and used his knowledge and experience of British administration to rid Britain of its most effective functionaries in Ireland, thus demoralizing British forces and paving the way for their defeat. One of his most valuable informers was Neligan, also a British civil servant, but working at Dublin Castle, headquarters of the British in Ireland.

Despite his daily work for the British administration, Neligan was avidly against British occupation of Ireland, so he volunteered to assist Collins secretly, initially by giving him personal details of British staff, including addresses and daily routines, later by organizing military or guerilla assaults on small groups and individuals.

When Collins was shot dead in August 1922 Neligan was promoted by Sinn Fein to Colonel. Later, from its inception, O'Higgins gave him responsibility for the detective section, 'G' squad, of the new Garda Síochana as Chief Superintendent. Neligan was cold-blooded and efficient, and was well known for his ruthless determination to see every 'contract' through to the end; he never undertook anything he could not complete.

Justice Minister O'Higgins had acted privately at the request of Mrs George Yeats, because Senator William Butler Yeats's Catholic republican working class lover had born him a son and could put his reputation under threat. He had privately contracted Garda Superintendent Leopold Dillon to ask Lily O'Neill to end her relationship with Yeats, and also to disclose her son's name and address.

On completion of his contract Dillon had reported directly to O'Higgins, knowing that he would be protected. O'Higgins then ordered Neligan to reconstitute the murder to hide the involvement of its perpetrators, and also to remove any link between Yeats and Lily. As before, for obvious reasons there is no direct evidence to confirm this, but circumstantial evidence (which will be explained later) make it quite clear who was responsible for what.

The inquest started by Coroner Brennan, plus all evidence he and Superintendent Reynolds had collected at the scene of the crime, was completely discarded. These two seasoned professionals were removed from the case completely. Later their names were used to produce false evidence, as will be shown.

There is no documentation available to prove these allegations because it happened secretly at Dublin Castle, headquarters of Garda Siochana. The police records of this case of ninety years ago have never been released, despite many requests. Such documentation does however still exist.[57]

All this took place within one week in early June 1925. Lily O'Neill was murdered at approximately 3am on 9th June. After Dillon and Purcell were taken into custody, the next seven months were spent interviewing witnesses and taking statements in order to eliminate unwanted evidence and edit events, by force if necessary. Dillon and Purcell were kept in custody from arrest until their trial, so that they were out of contact with the public enraged by the murder, and so that the Chief Superintendent could school them in their new stories.

Neligan's role was complicated. He had to exonerate Justice Minister O'Higgins, Superintendent Dillon and Peace Commissioner Dr. Purcell, whilst preserving the reputation of the Free State to avoid British interest in the case and any subsequent attempt to take over control of the state. It was also imperative to eliminate any involvement of Senator Yeats or his wife, which meant hiding from public view the real identity of Honor Bright and her son. The easiest way of doing this was to reconstitute her as a prostitute, since this would make her socially unacceptable and below public or political recognition.

After Dillon gave himself up admitting that he had killed Honor Bright, O'Higgins told George and Yeats immediately.

Yeats's severe grief and depression, referred to by Senator Joseph Hone as "heart troubles"[58] dates from this time.

O'Higgins and Neligan devised a new plot making Lily a prostitute. Such a story would eliminate suspicion of the Free State and O'Higgins, since prostitution was seen as due to impoverishment of Irish families, caused by the British before the instigation of the Free State. It would also remove Kevin as Yeats's heir: if his mother was a prostitute anyone could be his father.

The objective for Yeats and his wife was to face down rumours. It was imperative that Yeats should stop having anything more to do with Kevin; he must disown him completely, otherwise the whole subterfuge would flounder. They were to project themselves as a traditional family and keep away from prying eyes or ears. Yeats must maintain political correctness; he had no choice in the matter, having been confronted with a fait accompli.

By this time the murder of Honor Bright held front-page headlines in every newspaper in Dublin; every section of society was intrigued. It was much easier to claim that it was a simply a random event with no consequences, the accidental murder of nobody important. This would protect the Garda and judiciary, and also remove the political stains. 1925 was an era of deference, and Lily was in the wrong section of society for judicial concern. Property law rather than love dictated marriage partnerships, so adultery was condoned provided it was discreet. However this was not simple adultery: Lily's son was in the care of a clever woman and her partner who both knew his father. They could be expected to tell the son to about his father as soon as he could understand. Madge Hopkins was in the same position.

Other people also knew of Yeats's son, since Yeats was well known for being straightforward; he had always up to now been an honest man. Maud certainly knew of Lily's pregnancy and its source, and so did Oliver St John Gogarty and John Quinn. All Dubliners were renowned for their curiosity, particularly about those with money, authority or glamour.

Knowing the father of Lily's child meant understanding the political aspects of this murder. A poor young Catholic nationalist woman having a secret affair with a comparatively rich, elderly, unionist Nobel prizewinner, world-famous poet and married Senator; was this how politicians in the new Free State acted? She had borne him a son before his wife had done so, so that the illegitimate one had more claim to his wealth than the legitimate one; was this an example of moral standards in the new Free State? The Senator's clandestine lover had been murdered by an officer of the Garda Síochana acting for the Minister of Justice, who was working secretly on behalf of the Senator's wife; was the whole Irish government corrupt?

But why did the case come to court at all? It would have been much less politically embarrassing to sack the perpetrators in disgrace with no pension, and give the victim's relatives compensation. A couple of small paragraphs in the newspaper would have been quite acceptable for the majority of people. It would have spared the reputation of the Ministry and the police if this murder could have been dealt with privately. But public interest was incredibly high and had to be calmed down. The simplest way to do this was to settle the case 'legally' so that no one was able to object.

Yeats wrote The Three Monuments in 1925 just after Lily's murder.

They hold their public meetings where
Our most renowned patriots stand,
One among the birds of the air,
A stumpier on either hand;
And all the popular statesmen say
That purity built up the State
And after kept it from decay;
Admonish us to cling to that
And let all base ambition be,
For intellect would make us proud
And pride bring in impurity:
The three old rascals laugh aloud.

This poem is about three unnamed fellow officials of the Free State, O'Higgins, O'Duffy and Neligan. In Yeats' opinion they are using the dignity of those who have upheld the state in the past ('our most renowned patriots'), usurping it to their own advantage. They hold sticks to bang the ground to bring attention to themselves ('a stumpier in either hand') so that people will listen to them saying that 'purity built up the State / And after kept it from decay'. They go further, saying that people should abandon 'base ambition' because being too clever, having too much 'intellect', will make us proud and susceptible to 'impurity'. However despite such fine, moral speeches, the metre, basic and plodding, and the last line of the poem show that Yeats holds them in contempt: they are 'three old rascals' with no morals, and they 'laugh aloud' at us.

This is the first poem Yeats has written in disgust about fellow politicians. Previously he had criticised Maud Gonne MacBride for her misguided devotion to a cause, but he never accused her of being a liar or fraud. He spent three years after Lily's murder facing down public criticism, concealing acute grieving and social embarrassment from public view and trying his best to live with his family.

The Tyrants That Spat

A public trial was arranged to impose authority on the wayward public and to give a patina of legal process in order to forestall political unease.

The court was held on 1st– 4th February 1926, outside the normal court circuit beginning on 16th February that year. So the court was illegal, a kangaroo court. Every legal official that appeared for the prosecution or on the judicial bench was hired privately by the Ministry of Justice using public taxes, as were the ancillary staff and the court building itself. Every day of the trial Neligan attended with other officers and sat with the public, watching closely. Each lawyer was given a specific role to play devised by Neligan at the request of O'Higgins. The whole trial was a sham created by the Garda Siochana for the Ministry of Justice.

The objective of the trial was to make Lily not worthy of consideration. She was publicly maligned in order to obscure the motive for her murder and remove all suspicion from George Yeats and O'Higgins, and to cover up the muddle in Yeats' private life. Moreover his illegitimate son had to be made insignificant, as did the mother, in order to protect Mrs Yeats. How could she be held to blame without involving O'Higgins? This trial did not have the objective of finding the truth; rather it was a thorough, ruthless whitewashing in order to conceal the truth.

Neligan accordingly eradicated all Lily's papers and other possessions from her rented room; he had all the authority he needed and enough power to brush aside anyone who objected. No one knows except the Garda whether her things were completely destroyed or whether some were kept in Garda Archives. Margaret McGill's possessions regarding Lily were also purged. She was coerced into silence about Kevin's real parents.[59]

The newspaper of 9th June 1925, the day Honor Bright's body was found, reported that her only possessions were some Woodbine cigarettes, a powder compact and puff, a few coins and a rosary. However one of the witness depositions differs. The Coroner, Dr J. P. Brennan, made his witness deposition on 14th June, a few days after O'Duffy had taken over the case, to report the state of the body when found.[60] However later, in Dublin Castle, headquarters of the Garda, Brennan's name was crossed off the document, and 'Superintendent John H. Reynolds', the name of the first policeman at the scene of the crime, was superimposed. Most of the testimony in the deposition given by Brennan remains unaltered, but there are several important alterations. On page two Brennan had written: "Photos A, B, C D produced." Later the word "Photos" was crossed out and substituted with the word "Exhibit", and the letters B, C and D were crossed out, so that it read: Exhibit A. All photos were removed from the case because they showed a decently clad, reputable young woman, not a prostitute.

It is written with the same type of pen and ink as Brennan had used, but in different handwriting; the writer cannot easily form the letters in the word.

On page three the Coroner had written,

"I searched the pockets. I found in them a pair of kid gloves, a handkerchief, a purse containing one shilling and five pennies, also in pocket a half-crown; a sixpenny bit and 7½d in coppers, a hair comb; a packet of 'Woodbine' cigarettes; one 'Player's' cigarette and three cigarette 'butts'. In the left hand of the deceased was the coloured handkerchief produced. There was an end of cigarette on her costume, a scent bottle and some loose matches. A face cream. Photo Exhibit A. Other articles...."

However the last three sentences have been crossed out and a less confident writer has added "a Box containing Amalthusian Sheath ~~were~~ was also in Pocket."[61]

In other words Photo A of the contents of her pockets was eliminated so that evidence of the original contents was lost forever, and the face cream tin was substituted for a box of condoms, reinforcing the claim that she was a prostitute. The police, headed by Neligan under orders from O'Higgins, were systematically and deliberately destroying evidence and substituting falsehoods before the trial. Neither Brennan nor Reynolds was aware of perjury in their depositions, since they were off the case and had no access to Dublin Castle.

After the Divorce Bill speech on June 11th 1925, which had been planned weeks ahead and could not be avoided, Yeats was out of circulation in every sphere of life. The dates of his absence were very precise: they began when Lily (Honor Bright) was murdered on Wednesday June 9th 1925, and continued until the week after the trial of her alleged murderers ended, on Friday February 4th 1926.

He was said to have "heart trouble" but according to his biographers he had no contact with doctors and no medical care. The poems that he wrote during this time were plentiful, but they were suddenly full of despair and grief. He quietly resumed management and direction of the Abbey Theatre from the following September, but did not appear in public until Monday 8th February 1926, when Sean O'Casey's play "The Plough and the Stars" was premiered for one week at the Abbey theatre. This production began immediately after the trial, as soon as the weekend was over.

The four-day trial of Purcell and Dillon took place at the Central Criminal Court in Green Street. It was north of the river Liffey, far away from Merrion Square, the Abbey Theatre and the Irish government buildings, and miles away from Catherine Street and the Coombe. The street was narrow, with a jail next door to house the defendants.

Kevin O'Higgins had chosen a good friend, a very expensive prosecutor to securely, irresistably bring the court and the jury to the conclusion he had planned in advance. Mr W. Carrigan K. C. had worked closely with the Minister of Justice on the Committee on the Court of Justice Act 1924. This was an Act of the Oireachtas (No. 10 of 1924) that established a new system of courts for the Irish Free State. Once the Act came into operation the courts previously established by the Parliament of the United Kingdom ceased to exist. In parallel with this process the revolutionary Dail Courts created during the civil war, for which Maud Gonne was a judge, were also wound up by Acts passed in 1923 and 1925. The entire legal system was the responsibility of O'Higgins, the Minister of Justice and External Affairs; he had complete control over every aspect of it.

On the first day the courthouse was crowded, and as the week progressed the crowds increased, so that by the end of the second day witnesses, Civic Guard and court officials were late for their appearances.[62] Each day reporters mentioned the presence of "several well-dressed ladies"[63] e.g. Mrs Sheehy-Skeffington, K. Barry and other republican women opposed to the Free State. The other notable group was medical professionals, although the mass of interested citizens far outweighed them.

Every newspaper, no matter of what persuasion, had sent a reporter. The general public viewed the case as scandalous, shameful and intensely political. It was widely known by the populace that Honor Bright had a son.

Both accused men pleaded not guilty to the charge of murder. Despite having given himself up the day after the murder, probably to O'Higgins who had given him his contract, Dillon's statement on being charged with the murder read

" ... I know nothing whatever about this charge."[64]

Dr. Purcell's counsel challenged six members of the jury, while Dillon's challenged none. Purcell had repeatedly asked to be released from custody during the investigation, and feared conviction despite his plea of innocence. Meanwhile Dillon, who had been divested of his uniform on being charged, had never requested release, knowing that he had friends in high places. But Purcell had none and therefore expected to be used as a scapegoat.

Mr. Carrigan, the chief prosecutor, described the murder as "extraordinary";[65] in his opinion such a "disgusting" tale could only be found "in the pages of neurotic fiction". The two accused were

"men who had hitherto held positions of standing and authority within the district".

Dillon had been " Chief Police Officer and Superintendent of Police in the Dunlavin district", with headquarters in Dunlavin and responsibility for Baltinglass, Donard and Blessington districts. His duty was to

"keep discipline, preserve order and do right and justice amongst all people".

Dillon's part-time contracts and his unofficial job as warden at Mountjoy prison were not mentioned. Purcell, Carrigan said, was a physician, surgeon and dispensary doctor at Blessington, as well as Peace Commissioner. He was described to the court as a

"young, successful and prosperous professional man".

Continued on page 101

William Butler Yeats in 1923 aged 57

Kevin Barry O'Neill in 1943 aged 22

The Falsified Witness Deposition

Coroner J. C. Brennan's witness deposition is on the following pages. He gave it to Chief Superintendent Neligan when ordered to relinquish responsibility for the investigation to him.

Neligan took it to Dublin Castle, the Garda Headquarters, and altered the witness name to 'Supt. John Reynolds', the first officer at the scene of the crime, before presenting it to the jury. It was not shown in open court.

Brennan and Reynolds were unaware of this, as they had both been taken off the case the day after the murder, and neither was given access to Dublin Castle. This false evidence was used to convince the judge, counsel and jury that 'Honor Bright' was a prostitute.

Police photographs were eliminated and not mentioned in court.

A condom in a box was added to her pocket, suggesting illegal, immoral and reprehensible actions.

In page 1 of Dr J. P. Brennan's (Coroner) witness deposition, the name has been altered to Superintendent John Reynolds.

In the last line of page 2, in 'Photos A, ~~B, C, D~~', the last three letters have been crossed out and 'Exhibit' added before A. It now reads: "Photos Exhibit A produced."

In page 3 *"Tin of face cream"* has been crossed out, and in its place *"... and in her pocket Amalthusian sheath..."* inserted. (I.e. a condom.)

Page 4 is a note containing cross-questioning by Mr Joseph O'Connor, S. C. (instructed by Mr McCarroll, solicitor, Wicklow) for Dr Purcell.

The Bullet

This bullet was found lodged behind the shoulder blade during the post-mortem of Lily O'Neill / Honor Bright. No matching gun was ever sought or located. The bullet is from a Browning revolver issued as standard to Belgian troops during the First World War. Therefore it incriminates Leopold J. Dillon, who was in Belgium in 1919-20.

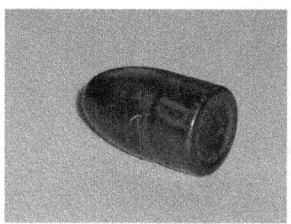

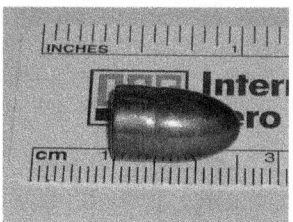

Leopold J. Dillon stated in court that he had no knowledge of firearms, and was a British 2nd Lieut. In fact he served in Belgium with the Artists Rifles, a private Army Officer training unit, having joined in 1919.

The Artists Rifles disbanded the following year, so that Dillon always remained a Private, though he had expected to become an officer. The Unit served at Mons in Belgium in its last tour of duty, and then became a part-time territorial unit. Therefore Dillon had opportunity to find and keep the Belgian Army gun used to shoot Lily O'Neill.

Margaret McGill standing outside the cellar of 2 Catherine Street near The Coombe in the Liberties, Dublin in 1922. She is holding Kevin 'McGill' in her arms. In that year Yeats and his family moved back from Oxford to Dublin, and Lily moved away from Catherine Street to 48 Newmarket, changing her name to Honor Bright from Lizzie O'Neill. Other photographs were probably taken at the same time, but none exist now.

Mrs McGill's partner

James White shared the cellar of 2, Catherine Street with his own son, Mrs McGill and Kevin. He had served in the Great War and died 1929-30 of sclerosis of the liver, although he never drank alcohol. Kevin, who knew him as his father, said he was 'the nicest, kindest man in the world'.

Garda Photographs of Lily O'Neill/Honor Bright

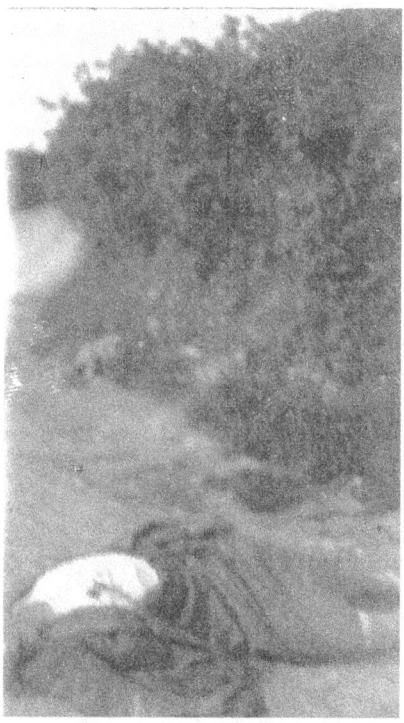

On this page and the next are shown photographs of Lily O'Neill taken by Sgt. Andrew Gordon, at the behest of Supt. John Reynolds, the first Garda officer at the scene of the murder on the morning of 9th June 1925. They were not used or mentioned in court during the trial.

The fourth photo of the contents of the murder victim's pockets was also not shown in court. Neligan destroyed the photo because it showed Lily's tin of face cream (as listed in Coroner Brennan's first inquest), which he substituted for a box of condoms.

This photograph shows Lily's modest, smart clothing. According to Coroner Brennan she had not been attacked or molested.

Continued from page 87

Carrigan emphasised the elevated status of each man and avoided any reference to their past. He did not mention Dillon's military service or his year of medical studies; he did not say he was twenty-five years old and unmarried. He failed to state that Purcell was a family man with no military or police service and hardly any experience with guns.

Carrigan then launched into melodramatic rhetoric to stress that the crime was of a sexual nature. The victim was "an unhappy girl of the unfortunate class" and the crime "a hideous tale of a night of debauchery, culminating in the deliberate and cold-blooded murder of one of the unhappy victims of their lust".

Prostitution and sexual immorality were highly contentious in the Free State. To Catholics it was morally indefensible; women who indulged were bound for Hell. To nationalists it was entirely a result of British occupation and had no place in a free Ireland. So the murder victim was summarily dismissed as a prostitute, the implication being that the fault lay with women of her type, rather than with silly lads led astray. She was merely "...one of... the victims..." and thus categorised, she had no personal value. The police photographs, which would have told a different story, were not used in court and no one was made aware that they existed.[66]

Carrigan was a master of manipulative rhetoric; he extolled the virtues of Dillon, describing him as "a Chief of Police, who, when he saw that suspicion fell on him, sat down and wrote an account...[which was] a complete collaboration of the evidence of witnesses..." Clearly such a man, he implied, was as honest and God-fearing as they come. He confirmed also the accurate account given by Purcell, but emphasised the "disgusting and horrible orgy", thus simultaneously smearing dirt on both the accused doctor and the victim.

He then went on to describe the victim, who had fallen on her right side "and was dressed in the clothes which she was seen to wear as late as three o'clock the same morning". He told the court she had been shot with "a bullet from a small pistol or revolver" but deliberately did not produce in court the bullet, which was in fact from a military revolver. It had struck her "on the right breast, close to the nipple ... and pierced her heart", killing her so suddenly that death was instantaneous and there was only a trace of blood.

"The woman", he alleged, "was one of those unhappy creatures who, not through choice, but through some cursed necessity, was compelled to seek her living on the streets at night". No evidence whatsoever was offered to back up this damaging assertion, no details of lifestyle, income, clients, pimps or daily routines at all. None of the outcomes of the very dangerous, stressful lifestyles of prostitutes in Dublin in 1925, such as neglect, abuse and physical or mental illness, were considered. Once again the police photographs would have proved this allegation false. Carrigan dismissed her from the case by presenting her as so corrupt and irredeemable that there was no need to discuss her any further. "For four years she had lived under the pseudonym of Honor Bright", he confided to the jury, "...For some time she had lived in lodging at Newmarket with a companion..."

The mysterious companion was never named or produced. There was never any attempt during the entire trial to discover the motive for the murder. Why she was murdered was never mentioned in court by lawyers or witnesses. Neligan had blocked this aspect of the investigation.

The female residents of the house in which she lived confirmed Lily's identity. One or two local people knew her as Lizzie O'Neill, but at her lodgings she was Honor Bright. The reasons for her changes of identity were not examined. The all-male jury was encouraged to imagine the victim as a streetwalker. When she went out on the night of the murder, said Carrigan,

"she was seen in the company of the two accused..."

so by implication she got what she deserved.[67]

Carrigan then sketched the movements of the two defendants on Monday 8th June and in the early hours of the next day. They met in Blessington after work, had a drink at the summer fair, borrowed civilian overcoats and set off for Dublin together in Purcell's car. After various engagements they met the victim and another girl at half past midnight outside the Shelbourne Hotel. Some time later Purcell, who by this time was very drunk on whisky, told Bridie that a girl wearing a grey dress had robbed him, and threatened to kill her, or if she eluded him, to kill a substitute. He had had a gun in his pocket.

Finally on the way home in the early hours they had met the murder victim

"...standing in the street where she had been left and persuaded her to go into the car again."

The gun was not mentioned at this point.

A little further on in Harold's Cross a policeman on night duty had seen a motorcar parked beside
"a dead wall and an overhanging hawthorn bush – a lonely spot. Standing on the pavement he saw a small man and a girl,

and on the road he saw a tall man who appeared to be bareheaded and to be wearing a tight-fitting coat. The girl was saying something very loudly and assertively; her voice indicated that she was very much in earnest about something. The constable walked across the road to get a full view and noticed that they immediately ceased speaking and hurried over to the motorcar. The girl as she was entering the car once again became assertive. In such a hurry were they to get into the car that the tall man stepped over the side into the driver's seat, whilst the smaller man and the girl entered by the door, which was immediately banged, and the car drove away to Ticknock."[68]

The policeman's evidence was dismissed as insufficient because he was asked to positively identify the two men, and declined. No reason was given: however he will have been aware of the professional consequences of identifying a former police superintendent and a former peace commissioner as guilty.

A couple in the vicinity of the murder that night had heard a shot, but they were not called as witnesses. Their testimony was unheard.

Carrigan manipulated the facts further. These men, he said,

"saw this unfortunate creature ... in the deserted streets and took her away ... Taking off her shoe ... to use it as a weapon of defence ... was the last and only chance of a defenceless and miserable woman when she saw herself in danger."

In his version she had fought to defend herself, though what against was not made clear. Being 'defenceless and miserable' she had failed.

"You will be asked," he said, "to hold without compunction that the evidence establishes a convincing case of guilt against the accused."

Yet since he had already convinced the jury that the girl was socially and morally ruined, her murder would be seen as merely a consequence of her behavior, regrettable but unavoidable.[69]

So the first day in court ended with Carrigan having established the sinfulness, corruption, depravity and miserable worthlessness of the 'unfortunate creature' contrasted with the silly, puerile behaviour of the 'lads'. The balance had been tipped in the defendants' favour.

On the second day

"long before the hour fixed for the resumption of the case, large numbers of people collected in knots outside the building."[70]

The first witness was James McCabe, a taxi driver in a rented vehicle, who had arrived on St Stephen's Green opposite the Shelbourne Hotel at 2.40am on the night of the murder. He had seen Purcell and Bridie in Purcell's grey two-seater car and they had asked him for change for a £1 note. He had overheard Purcell's words about the theft of his money by "a tall girl with bobbed hair", and had also seen Dillon and Honor beside the grey car.

He then saw the other taxi-cab drawing up, Honor walking quickly towards it and being driven away at about 3.15 am. After this he saw the grey car containing the two defendants also drive off.

He was not asked to say in which direction the grey car drove off, or whether it was following the taxi. At no point was he asked what the defendants or the women had said, nor was he asked about their moods, emotions or general demeanour. He explained that he had been standing beside Dillon and Honor for at least half an hour, but was not questioned about what had taken place between them. He was allowed only to confirm Purcell's words about the alleged theft and to confirm the locations of the four people, that is, who was where, when. No witnesses were asked open questions or allowed to give their own opinions.

Purcell's defence solicitor, the eminent, well-known Mr Joseph O'Connor, then asked him, "Did he [the taxi-driver] seem to want to pick her up?" to which the only possible answer was affirmative. Again this gave a skewed interpretation to the evidence: it implied that he wanted to pick her up because he intended evil deeds, and he was not allowed to clarify. The question had been put in order to make the jury suspicious of him.

The next to testify was the other taxi-driver, who owned his vehicle.

"Ernest Woodruff, taxi driver and owner, stated that about 2.30 a.m. on June 9 he saw Honor Bright and another girl talking to two men in a grey two-seater motor at the archways opposite the Shelbourne Hotel. He had seen the women before and knew Honor's name.

"Honor Bright came up to him, and then went back to the motor car. He heard her say to one of the men, "I'll see you again", and the man replied, "All right". She then went into his car, and he drove her to Leonard's corner, via Harcourt Street. They stopped on the way near the railway arch, Harcourt

Road, and Honor Bright got out for a few minutes. At Leonard's corner she left his car, and he last saw her standing on the footpath at Leonard's corner. "[71]

He reversed his car and was heading back when he spotted the grey two-seater driving towards her. There were two men in the car, one of whom was Purcell, whom he had seen sitting in the car on the Green.

"At this stage the witness was about to relate a conversation which he had had with the deceased in connection with a statement made by her that she was afraid she was being shadowed to Leonard's corner, when Mr Moore objected on the grounds that a conversation that had taken place was not evidence."[72]

Woodruffe was asked whether he had ever seen him before then, but answered never. The implication of the question was that Woodruffe knew Purcell and did not want to admit it.

O'Connor re-examined Woodruffe about Honor Bright. Under questioning Woodruffe said that he knew Honor by sight because he had "picked her up on the Green" before, though he had never been introduced to her.[73] She, not knowing him well, had addressed him as "Jimmy", an informal name akin to 'mate', in Dublin. O'Connor's implication was that she was a prostitute using taxis at night for trade and that Woodruffe had been only too pleased to pick her up. No other reason for her using taxis was touched upon. Since he did not accuse Woodruffe directly, his tacit accusation could not be denied.

The second inquest in August the previous year had also related the above, but with one difference, that was not allowed to be mentioned in the trial that took place the following February, as the following report showed.

"At this stage the witness [Woodruffe] was about to relate a conversation which he had had with the deceased in connection with a statement made by her that she was afraid she was being shadowed to Leonard's corner, when Mr Moore objected on the grounds that a conversation that had taken place was not evidence.

The Coroner said that his Court was different from a Criminal Court or any other Court. All the jury was there for was to find the cause of the death of this girl, and he was prepared to admit any evidence that would assist the jury.

COURT CLEARED

Mr Moore again objected, and pointed out that hearsay evidence appearing in the press would affect his clients. In the circumstances he would ask the Coroner to clear the court, including even the police.

The Coroner said he was prepared to do so, but he would not exclude the Press if they undertook not to report what took place in the interval.

> The Press representatives present declining to give an undertaking not to report evidence given in their presence then retired from the Court with the members of the public and police officers.

After a brief interval the public and others were readmitted.[74]"

O'Connor then asked Woodruffe to relate the events of the whole evening, asking if he drank and implying that he was circling the town aimlessly in his car. " Were you trying to pick up girls instead?" Woodruffe answered "No," but O'Connor nevertheless continued to imply that he was an unreliable character with ulterior motives, openly doubting the witness's version of events.

After the murder Woodruffe had been arrested and detained from Saturday 13th to Wednesday 17th June before being released. There was no evidence against him but he had been treated as a suspect. In court O'Connor did his best to imply that Woodruffe had actually shot Honor, asking him when he had left the British Army - Woodruffe had never enlisted - whether he had ever owned a British Army gun, whether he had ever shown such a gun to another witness, and whether he had ever possessed ammunition.

In tacit implications O'Connor was accusing Woodruffe of telling lies. He finished by implying that prostitutes fascinated the taxi-owner, who was asked if he knew Bridie, and how many other "girls on the town" he knew, to which Woodruffe answered one called Nora, whom he had driven in his cab. When Mr. Carrigan questioned him accusingly about whether there was any truth in the rumour that he had murdered Honor Bright, Woodruffe answered "None".

After lunch Mr O'Connor recalled Woodruffe, and once again accused him of lying, but this time about a separate incident. Woodruffe had stated that he had not driven his taxi between the night of the murder and Wednesday of the following week, when he was released from the police station. This was proven untrue in court since he had been seen driving on Thursday 11th June in the early hours. Whilst this had no impact on the case it served to make the jury more wary of his evidence. The case for the Crown closed at 4.15 pm.

Once again the questioning had concentrated on the movements of the witnesses and defendants, to the exclusion of facts which would have been far more revealing. Woodruffe was never allowed to state how Honor Bright had looked when he saw her, why she had approached him, what she had said to him, or why he had immediately agreed to take her home.

He was never asked why she wanted to go home, how much

the fare was or whether she had paid it. He was never asked whether they had talked, or to describe her mood during the car journey. In particular most of the evidence he had given in his deposition was not mentioned; in fact O'Connor had deliberately confused him so that he did not remember what he had previously declared.

The court never heard that he said to her as she approached his car, "What's wrong?", or that she stopped the taxi after passing under the railway bridge, got out and nervously looked down the road behind them, smoked a cigarette and said she thought they were being followed. Woodruffe was also never asked where he had dropped her or why.

Not only did O'Connor ignore his deposition; his intense, accusatory questioning deliberately prevented his witness from telling the truth. Neligan, by means of O'Connor, was intentionally constructing a case against him, making the jurors doubt his words, because he was the most dangerous witness. He knew detailed information about Honor's motives and fears that night, so he had to be silenced. The legal structure and Garda were being used to smear his name, cast doubt on his evidence and plant suspicion. The police force and lawyers in court were acting together to pervert the course of justice.[75]

The third day of the trial, Wednesday 3rd February, saw Dr. Purcell called to give evidence on his own behalf. Mr. O'Connor asked him to relate the events of the night of the murder, and Purcell swore that his account was accurate.

At about 1am on the morning of Tuesday 9th June he had picked up Dillon at the Sherbourne Hotel, intending to drive home. They had met two girls outside on the edge of St Stephen's Green, opposite the hotel. He had gone up Hume

Street with Bridie while Dillon stayed on the Green with Honor Bright. His declaration of having been robbed "was pure bravado" and he did not remember ever having threatened to kill anyone. He said had had no revolver but his stethoscope had been in his back pocket.

Another witness had seen him arriving home at about 4.30am and climbing in through the study window, after which he ate sandwiches and drank milk before going into his wife's bedroom and undressing, as she had testified. "He swore that he knew absolutely nothing about Honor Bright's murder."[76]

Purcell was never asked why he had gone to Dublin. His deposition had stated clearly that he had had no intention of doing so; that he had gone there because Dillon had said his motorcycle was not working and he wanted a lift in Purcell's car. Dillon had asked him while Purcell was on duty at the police station, then again just after work when they were both at the festival in Blessington. Dillon had said the festival was boring so they should go to Dublin for entertainment, and Purcell had agreed.

Purcell said he had fetched his car and picked up Dillon who had borrowed a civilian overcoat to wear over his uniform. On the way to Dublin they had stopped at a local pub, borrowed another civilian overcoat for Purcell and eaten a meal. Near Dublin Purcell had stopped at Naas for an hour or more to visit a retired doctor.

In Dublin they had met with two other women and had a meal and had sex with them afterwards. Purcell had spent money on them. All of them had drunk a lot of alcohol that evening, mostly whisky, starting early. Dillon had disappeared for a while to see his friend, but nobody in court wanted to know whom he had met. He and Dillon had agreed to meet later at the Shelbourne Hotel.[77]

Purcell was never asked his impression of Honor Bright's appearance, what she said or did, or the relationship between her and Dillon, although Purcell said he was in the car for at least an hour with the two of them. Nor was he asked how or why the two women had been waiting outside the hotel for him and Dillon. O'Connor's questions again implied that the women were streetwalkers touting for business.

In reality Purcell had a long-standing relationship with Bridie, as discovered by Justice Minister O'Higgins (or by Chief Supt. Neligan acting on his behalf). O'Higgins or Neligan had instructed Dillon to ask Purcell to bring along Bridie's friend to meet Dillon. Dillon will have described her to Purcell, to imply that he had seen her and fancied her in order to ensure that this particular girl would appear. In fact Purcell had never seen Honor Bright before, and she and Bridie had never seen Dillon before, but this was not made clear to the jury.

When Purcell had given his testimony a few other witnesses were called to give evidence relating to details of his submission, but added little to the proceedings apart from reinforcing O'Connor's implications of Purcell's and Woodruffe's guilt. Mrs Traynor stated that she had once seen Woodruffe with a revolver, which was hardly surprising since at least half the population owned one after the recent civil war. Captain Hornidge, Purcell's neighbour, had practised shooting with him eleven months before the murder. Purcell, he stated, turned up with a matching set of revolvers, one of which did not work. Jane Hamilton, a barracks attendant at Blessington, heard the car coming from Dublin direction at the same time as she, unable to sleep, heard the church clock at 4.25am.

Purcell's wife testified that she heard her husband come home just after half past four. She had given him twenty-five or thirty shillings the day before, and had seen his revolver in a small drawer that day, after her husband had left for Dublin. A Corporation street cleaner noticed nothing unusual outside the Shelbourne Hotel at 3.30am on Tuesday morning. An agent for Swift cars, like Purcell's, had timed the journey from Blessington to Dublin and stated that it took one hour and ten minutes. Dr Murphy of Naas said that Purcell visited him regarding a professional matter that Monday evening. The publican in Blessington stated that he lent Purcell two pounds at about 8 pm. With these small details the evidence concerning Dr Purcell was closed.[78]

Dillon was then called up to the witness box. He stated to O'Connor that his account of the events of the fateful night was accurate, although he was unsure of exact times.

On leaving the Sherbourne Hotel at 12.30 am with Dr Purcell he met the two girls on the Green and began to talk to them. Purcell left with Bridie while he talked to the other girl, Honor, at the corner for ten minutes before they got into the car.

The car was stationary for twenty minutes before they drove around the Green. He gave Honor all the loose change he had.

Some time later a taxi drew up, whereupon Honor got out of the car, shouted "Stop Jimmy!" and went away in the taxi. He did not see Honor again that night. He thought somebody with grey hair was in the back of the taxi.

He stated that he had no quarrel with Honor. Later he picked up Purcell and drove away with him. At some point he passed a cab and an occupant shouted "Good night!" They drove straight to Blessington and reached it about 4 am. At no point in the evening was he at Harold's Cross Road. He never had any firearm that evening.[79] Dillon's story was exactly the same as Purcell's.

Cross-examined by the Prosecutor, Mr Carrigan, Dillon stated that he had served with the British Army for one year, leaving in 1917 with the rank of second lieutenant but with no experience of firearms. After leaving he became a medical student at Cork University but left before qualifying and joined the Civic Guard.

He said he never wore uniform when travelling to Dublin, and on June 8th he changed out of uniform because of the intense heat of the day. He hoped to have some dinner, visit a theatre and return home afterwards. However after dinner it was too late to visit the theatre. He admitted that Honor had asked him to drive her home, and he had refused because the car did not belong to him.

Yet again, the omissions in his evidence were far more eloquent than his statements. He was not questioned at all about what had occurred before midnight, so the fact that he had personally arranged the trip to Dublin was not clear to the jury, nor that it was his idea to borrow other people's mufti overcoats despite the overwhelming heat of the day. He was not asked why he needed such camouflage.

He was not asked whether the meeting was pre-arranged, whether he was aware of the affair between Purcell and Bridie, or whether he had specifically told Purcell to bring Honor to the meeting.

Lawyers also did not enquire what Dillon and Honor had said to each other in the first ten minutes or during the twenty minutes in the car, what had happened when the car was stationary, or why he had begun driving around the Green with her in the car. By this point the jury would have assumed that they were having sex, because they had repeatedly been told that she was a prostitute, and driving around the Green late at night was what some prostitutes did. The jury was allowed to assume they had sex in the car.

His exact route was never requested, or the subject of their conversation, or what was said or done inside the car for over an hour.

Dillon stated that he gave her money but he was not asked how much or why. She was found with just over five shillings in her pocket in small change. However a prostitute would have charged ten shillings or more per hour; a note rather than coins would have been expected, and a night's earnings would have been more appropriate. There was no evidence other than his statement that her small change came from him.

Her reason for wanting to go home was not requested. Dillon's reason for refusing to drive her home was accepted without demur, even though she lived only ten minutes' drive away, and he had already been driving without Purcell for at least an hour.

Woodruffe's evidence of what Honor Bright said and her emotional state was not produced in court because Dillon's defence lawyer, Geoghegan, haf objected on the grounds that it would injure his client's case.[80] The taxi owner would have stated that Honor was afraid of something when she approached his taxi on the Green, so that he asked her "What's wrong?" and when he took her home she thought she was being followed.[81] Any threat to her must have come from Dillon, who spent all the evening with her after midnight, and whose company she was fleeing when she ran away towards the taxi. Dillon was not questioned about this at all.

The duration of the drive around the Green was not questioned in court. The original post-mortem had stated that sexual activity had not taken place, and Honor did not look in disarray when found; so what had been said, and why had he spent an hour with her driving around St Stephen's Green, yet refused to drive her home? This of course was the reason that the original post-mortem was not produced in court.

Woodruffe saw Dillon driving the car that followed his taxi, with Purcell in the passenger seat. The police constable on night duty saw him and Purcell at Harold's Cross on the road to Ticknock, talking with Honor, who was speaking loudly and earnestly. Dillon was not cross-questioned about any of this.

Dillon's statement that he had not been in possession of a firearm on the 8th and 9th of June was also accepted without demur, even though it was highly unusual for any police officer to be without a gun at any time. It was part of the daily uniform, given the recent volatile civil war in Ireland. In any case, in the turmoil of the Free State no ex-army policeman would have been promoted so quickly to a senior position in charge of three districts without an appropriate knowledge of arms.

Incredibly, the court accepted without question that a commissioned officer being trained for trench warfare in the First World War should have no experience of guns. Every army recruit receives weapons training with guns. Dillon had claimed to be a Second Lieutenant, and although he was not, he had certainly had military training for that role, and as an officer-to-be had been issued with a revolver rather than a rifle.

However the dates he gave for his Army service were not true. He did not join the British Army until 1919, after the Great War had ended. His company was the Artists' Rifles, an officer training corps where entry was restricted to recommended recruits from universities. The battalion ended the war at Marmignies, south of Mons, Belgium, and was disbanded in 1920, so Dillon always remained a Private; therefore his claim to have been a Second Lieutenant was also perjury.[82]

However he had shot and murdered Lily judging from the method of shooting, common among soldiers at that time, of aiming in the dark at a cigarette. As Dillon must have had a gun it is not surprising that Lily got into Purcell's car after Woodruffe's taxi had disappeared.

In addition Dillon had not changed out of his uniform, merely covered it with an overcoat on the hottest day of the year. He had done this to conceal his gun and uniform.

Dillon stated that he was going to Dublin to see a fellow officer, but he was not asked who or what they discussed. He met with Justice O'Higgins, since he went to Sandy Cove where O'Higgins lived. But the jurors were not told this.

The bullet found at post-mortem, just below Honor's left shoulder blade, was not produced or identified in court. It was a short nine-millimetre brass bullet from a Browning pistol, the military semi-automatic model produced at the Fabrique Nationale in Belgium from 1903, standard issue to Belgian troops during the Great War. Therefore Dillon, who had fought with the Artists Rifles in France and Belgium, had brought it home. He would also have had experience with it in his army and police work.

One wonders if these omissions constituted the "startling revelations and surprising turns which the trial took during its course"[83], as reported by the press. Although the questioning of Woodruffe had taken an entire day, questioning each of the accused took only half a day, and the State Prosecutor did not put any questions to them.

The fourth and final day of the trial dawned on Thursday 4th of February 1926 and began about 2 pm. The High Court in Green Street Courthouse was packed tightly the whole day. By shortly after five o'clock the two solicitors representing Dr Purcell and Leopold Dillon had each pleaded their clients' lack of culpability.

When Mr Carrigan, K.C. stepped forward to make the final prosecution address to the jury, " the courthouse was packed tighter than at any time during the day. At the back of the gallery people were standing five or six deep, and it is doubtful if any of these could even hear counsel's speech, much less see him. But those who managed to gain admittance to the precincts of the court considered themselves fortunate. Outside the locked gates of the building surged a big crowd, which gave the police no little difficulty in keeping order. At every possible opportunity they ran over to the gates and pleaded, in most cases vainly, to get in."

"Meantime, inside the court, Mr Carrigan was presenting his case to the jury, and during the hour and a quarter which he spoke, dead silence reigned. When he finished about 20 minutes to 7 o'clock, and the judge prepared to sum up, the atmosphere was tense. Then a little restless stir ran around the people present, and then they settled down again to listen."

"For over two hours Mr Justice Sullivan addressed the jury, goung through the evidence carefully and advising them on points of law. He concluded, with no little spirit, that in the eyes of the law this poor girl, Honor Bright, occupied the same position as the first lady in the land, and it would offer her the same protection. And in the case of murder, the full resources of the law would be brought into operation, as this case evidenced."

"The jury then retired, only to be recalled some minutes later for the judge to direct their attention to a certain period of time. This was at the request of Mr O'Connor [Purcell's counsel]."

By this time the clock showed just after 9 pm, an unusually late hour for the conclusion of such a prominent trial as this one. Everyone waiting inside and outside the courtroom, whether onlooker or official, witness or accused, was extremely tense and very tired. It was expected that the jury would take some hours to reach its verdict. Reporters were therefore aghast at the speed with which the jury reappeared.

"Many of the people were attempting to make their way out of the court, and just as everybody was ‚,taking it easy' the door of the jury-box opened and the jury filed in after about three minute's absence. Then there was a tremendous rush and bustle, counsel came rushing back, the officials ran all over the place, the judge then sat and silence reigned. Then the Clerk of the Peace said, "Have you considered your verdict, gentlemen?" "Yes." Then the Clerk read out the verdict: "Not guilty". The decision was unanimous. Then the judge, turning to the prisoners, said "You are discharged."

Coroner Brennan had reported Honor Bright to be an innocent, respectable victim of a heinous crime who had been suddenly shot, her body and clothing untouched; the first person to see the corpse at 7am had said she looked as if she had fallen asleep; but neither was called to give evidence. The photos support this composed, undisturbed posture and show that her shoe had simply slipped off her foot. But the court was never told of the existence of the photographs.

Madge Hopkins lived at the same address as the victim, had known her for five years and therefore knew that she had a child, and that her son had not been given away or adopted. Moreover she had been with Honor on the night of her murder. Nevertheless she said nothing about this in her deposition or in court; she had somehow been forced into silence.

All documentary evidence from Lily, such as her letters, books, address book, diary and birth certificates for herself and her son, was discarded or eliminated. None of her possessions were used or referred to in court.

Furthermore several other witnesses to the crime were not called forward. The couple that had heard the shot in the early hours was not called to give evidence. The Garda constable on night duty that had seen the two men and the woman quarrelling was allowed to give evidence, but the identities of the people and the car involved were not confirmed, so his evidence was discarded. The man who had found the victim was not called to give evidence, nor the first policemen at the scene or the coroner. The absence of these witnesses obscured the character of the victim and altered her identity to that of a prostitute. It also obscured the identity of the killers.

The later post-mortem report was falsified in order to malign the victim. Dr. O'Mahoney, working directly for Chief Superintendent Neligan, declared that the handkerchief in the victim's hand had semen on it and there was a "whitish discharge" from the vagina, which was not further identified, but the wording used implied recent sexual intercourse, as did the semen on the handkerchief. None of these had been seen at the first inquest conducted by Brennan, so they were falsehoods invented under the authority of Neligan. The new post-mortem did not state that she had given birth.

Many people who knew the victim were excluded from the trial, and those that were called up were not allowed to state relevant details about her life. All witness depositions were very short and missed out many important facts such as all speech and emotions of the victim, the existence of her son, the foster-mother and family he lived with.

No evidence was allowed about Honor Bright except her home address, age and where she came from. Witnesses were not even allowed to state how they had met her. Locations of the two accused, the taxi-drivers and Bridie took precedence over words spoken. Motives were of no interest to the court at all.

Madge Hopkins or Bridie, Lily's best friend, stated that she had known 'Lizzie' for five years in 1925, but did not state in court that they had met the year that Lizzie gave birth to Yeats' son. They had recently resided in separate rooms at the same women's lodging house, 48 Newmarket, but this was not made clear to the court.

The two young women may well have had similar circumstances; they became good friends and knew a lot about each other. For example, Madge knew that Lizzie came from County Carlow, and that she received letters addressed to Lily O'Neill despite being currently known as Honor Bright. She also knew how long she had lived at her current address and where she had lived previously. She therefore knew that Lizzie had a son, and where he and the foster-family lived, just two streets away.

Madge may even have lived at 2 Catherine Street while Lizzie lived there; they may have shared the same large family room in the semi-derelict eighteenth century mansion, now a tenement, since single women with children did not have much choice of accommodation. Therefore she had seen Yeats calling to see Lizzie and her son. She probably knew him as Michael, Mick or Mike. Yeats states that he knew Madge and Margaret in one of his poems.[84]

Nevertheless when she appeared as a witness in court she said none of this. All that she stated was directly in response to questioning, and the closed questions were carefully curtailed to hide evidence about Lily's circumstances. Lily's child and the foster-mother's address, the name under which her child was known and the identity of his father were not mentioned at all. Madge also made no attempt to mention any of these people, so she was forced to keep her mouth shut.[85]

Dissenting witnesses were also not called forward and not referred to in court. Margaret McGill, Kevin's foster mother, had been silenced in some way, as had her partner James White. Neither was asked or allowed to give a witness deposition, or called to attend court.[86]

The speed of the four-day trial meant there was no time for consideration or reassessment. The last day started at 2pm and finished at 9pm (with a break from 5 to 6.30pm) on Thursday 4th February 1925. No opportunity for appeal was considered.

The two accused were acquitted.

After the verdict there were no newspaper reports about any aspects of the murder, the victim or the trial. The whole case was over and completely taboo; no one was allowed to discuss it further or complain. The Garda made sure of that.

Red wine and dirt had been spilt on the new white carpet, but a white rug had been stretched over the top; no stain was evident on the new Free State.

The public was in uproar at the injustice they observed, but in the face of Garda opposition little could be said in public. The trial ended by acquitting the accused despite obvious guilt. The Garda silenced newspapers as soon as the trial ended, to discourage further objections.

All involvement of Yeats, George and O'Higgins was hidden from the public and the courtroom. Neither the court nor the newspapers ever mentioned Honor Bright's son or his foster-mother. Yeats disowned his illegitimate son and George's son inherited his property.

Oedipus' Child Descends into the Loveless Dust

Dublin in the 1920s was a small city with little traffic. Most people walked everywhere, whatever their status. 2 Catherine Street, where Mrs Magill, James, his son and Kevin lived, was southeast of the river Liffey near the Coombe, the main street in the Liberties. The tenement was an 18th century mansion that had crumbled and rotted over the century as it was rented out, one family per room. It was in the poorest part of Dublin, outside the original city. People often passed each other in the street and said hello, and everyone was quick to recognise people who were new to the area.

From 1919 to 1922 Yeats and his family had a house in the southwest of the city near the law courts, university, parks and clubs at 73 Stephen's Green. He had rented it to Maud Gonne while they lived in Oxford. When Yeats was visiting Dublin he would reside at the United Arts Club nearby. It was only twenty minutes walk to Catherine Street. Lily would have known where Yeats lived before he moved to England.

In 1922 after the Free State was established, Yeats, George and their two children moved back to Dublin permanently and took a house at 82 Merrion Square. When this happened Lily changed her address from 2 Catherine Street to 48 Newmarket, beside a police station, and changed her name to Honor Bright. From Yeats's address the Abbey Theatre was just across the main bridge of the Liffey. When he became Senator Yeats he gained access to the politicians' club, The Hibernian in St Stephen's Green. It was still only twenty minutes walk to Lily's address.

Yeats had hired Mrs Magill as Kevin's foster-mother, at Gogarty's suggestion, and had paid for her midwifery skills. She had therefore realised that he was the father of Lily's son. Caring for this baby as her own son gave her great insight into all their relationship problems. It was inevitable that Lily, who was living above Mrs McGill before, during and for two years after the birth, should pour out her heart to Kevin's mother–figure when in pain, upset or depressed.

Through Lily, her best friend Madge Hopkins knew Yeats, Mrs Magill and Kevin, and she knew about Lily's second change of name and understood the reason for it. She recommended Lily's new address to all three adults, since she already lived there; they may have moved there together from Catherine Street. At any rate, both she and Yeats knew each other well.

After Lily's murder Mrs McGill and Madge continued to pass each other in the street; one can imagine the looks and emotions exchanged when words were forbidden. After the trial ended Yeats abandoned Kevin and stopped payments to Mrs McGill; since Kevin had been camouflaged as her own son, she could not prove that Yeats was the father. Yeats took up his work as senator again; newspapers reported that he had recovered from his 'heart problem'. In fact he had been suffering from severe grief.

Since George was Yeats's editor the dates of his poems are doubtful. In "Two Songs from a Play" the first song was supposedly written in May 1925, but Lily was murdered on June 9th that year. He speaks of his immense grief at her death, which "tore the heart out of his side And bear that beating heart away." One can assume that in reality he was speaking after her death.

The title poem of "The Tower" was written on 7th October 1925, four months after the Lily's murder, when his illegitimate son was four years old. His romantic, partly ruined, seasonally uninhabitable house was called Thoor (Tower) Ballylee. It is also a Tarot card predicting collapse, disaster and ruin. Yeats, master of the occult, was aware of both connotations, and the poet would have used both meanings.

In 'The Tower' Yeats's mood is dramatically changed from all previous publications. Despite his Nobel Prizes, Senator status, political functions, and successful poetry, he is suddenly suffering from depression, failure and fatigue. All at once his body feels old and he is conscious that people are laughing at him. He talks directly of his own self for the first time: "this absurdity" his body, "…this decrepit age…" and his "troubled heart". He says that he "must bid the Muse go pack", he can no longer write poetry because he has lost his ability to deal "in abstract things" and dare not express his feelings because he will "…be derided by / A sort of battered kettle at the heel".

In other words he is being sneered at and has become a laughing stock because of circumstances he cannot talk about in public. However his predicament was known to at least his own circle of friends including his wife George, Kevin O'Higgins and Joseph Hone, David Neligan, Maud, Gogarty, Bethel Solomons, Iseult and Francis Stuart, and also Margaret McGill and James White, to name but a few.

The second stanza repeats this expression of social "ruin" and failing "foundations" with the "…tree, like a sooty finger…" pointing accusingly at him "under the day's declining beam'" The blackness of the soot and the twilight reveal that he feels dirtied, blackened by recent events for which he holds himself responsible.

He paces upon the ruined roof, along the battlements and calls upon "images and memories… For I would ask a question of them all."

Yeats tells of a well-to-do neighbour, Mrs French. Her faithful, devoted serving-man had pre-empted his lady's wish and cut off the ear of a tenant farmer because he was "insolent", then delivered it to her "in a little covered dish". Yeats is referring to his wife, under the guise of Mrs French. George had made her wishes concerning Lily and her son very clear to O'Higgins, without giving him specific orders.

Like Mrs French's servant, O'Higgins had the power to carry out her desires, and he did so without consulting her in advance, producing a pleasing surprise, a fait accompli. Like Mrs French, George did not praise the action, since that would have meant accepting responsibility for it; but neither did she complain, being very happy with the result. Like O'Higgins, the servant continued as before with no admonition or blame, since his employer did not accuse him, and the farmer and others like him were afraid of the consequences if they did so. Only Yeats who was affected by this action; like Mrs French's farmer, Yeats had no say in it at all.

Yeats's next three stanzas tell of a "country wench" who sang so beautifully and innocently that men "…jostled…" to see her, but

"music had driven their wits astray…And one was drowned in the great bog of Cloone."

She had a disastrous effect on those around her because of her innocence and beauty. Just like Helen of Troy and Lily, she had "...all living hearts betrayed..." by inadvertently causing death.

"The tragedy began with Homer that was a blind man,"

just as Yeats had been blind to the consequences of his own actions.[87]

The next three stanzas tell of a character invented by Yeats twenty years before, just as Michael Robartes had been; Hanrahan was an old man who drank too much and was suicidal. In his younger days

"He so bewitched the cards under his thumb / That all but the one card became / A pack of hounds and not a pack of cards, / And that he changed into a hare."

Suddenly all the characters in Yeats's life had changed into a pack of hounds chasing after Lily, a delicate, frightened wild hare, to kill her. And like Hanrahan he was sure he had 'bewitched' all this with his adultery.

Yeats imagines tough men-at-arms in the castle. He summons all these characters to appear, but then dismisses everyone except Hanrahan. In his youth the old man had been a red-haired schoolteacher of intense passion; but he had been condemned for eternity when a fairy queen destroyed his life.

Yeats describes himself as just like Hanrahan, a

"half-mad rhapsodic poet, a failed seducer of real women and a great curser of old age". He is chased by the "hounds", a "man drowned in a bog's mire / When mocking Muses chose the country wench."

George was a Londoner, not a country wench, while Maud and Iseult lived in Paris and Dublin; so this had to refer to Lily from County Carlow.

Hanrahan, like Yeats, has been

'A lecher with a love on every wind...' who understands every '...plunge...into the labyrinth of another's being ...'.

Therefore he he has enough experience to answer Yeats's burning question,

'Does the imagination dwell the most / On a woman won or a woman lost?'

Who is most important, he asks, George or Lily? The time of writing of this poem tells us that the 'woman lost' was Lily, for it was written just after her murder. The 'woman won' is a synonym for a wife.

In the last stanza Yeats or Hanrahan answers his own question with despair.

"If on the lost, admit you turned aside From a great labyrinth out of pride,
Cowardice, some silly over-subtle thought
Or anything called conscience once;
And if that memory recur, the sun's
Under eclipse and the day's blotted out."[88]

This grief is expressed in 'A Man Young and Old', the title of which refers to himself, judging by the number of times he uses the word 'I'. It is part of 'The Tower" published in 1926, though the given date is 1927, a series of linked poems that tell the story of his relationship with Lily. Yeats seems to have stipulated the order in which these poems are presented, so that George was limited to editing individual words.

A Man Young and Old

I   First Love

Though nurtured like the sailing moon
In beauty's murderous brood,
She walked awhile and blushed awhile
And on my pathway stood
Until I thought her body bore
A heart of flesh and blood.

But since I laid a hand thereon
And found a heart of stone
I have attempted many things
And not a thing is done,
For every hand is lunatic
That travels on the moon.

She smiled and that transfigured me
And left me but a lout,
Maundering here and maundering there,
Emptier of thought
Than the heavenly circuit of its stars
When the moon sails out.

The first of the series is for a girl who is now dead, who '…blushed awhile…' and was as beautiful as '…the sailing moon…' She was '…In beauty's murderous brood…', her beauty had been the cause of her downfall.

The most likely destiny for beautiful girls in early 20th century

Ireland was a pre-marital pregnancy that would rob them of respectability, marriage and career and turn them into 'fallen women'; beauty was a lifetime's curse.

In the third poem he tells of a hedonistic 'Mermaid' who "…forgot in cruel happiness /That even lovers drown."

In the first poem and the second, "Human Dignity", Yeats refers to the girl as a 'stone' (as in 'Colonus' Praise'), 'a scene upon a painted wall', a theatrical sham, as she is now dead and only exists in his mind.

II   Human Dignity

Like the moon her kindness is,
If kindness I may call
What has no comprehension in't
But is the same for all
As though my sorrow were a scene
Upon a painted wall.

So like a bit of stone I lie
Under a broken tree.
I could recover if I shrieked
My heart's agony
To passing bird, but I am dumb
From human dignity.

III   The Mermaid

A mermaid found a swimming lad,
Picked him for her own,
Pressed her body to his body,
Laughed, and plungiing down
Forgot in cruel happiness

That even lovers drown.

He tells us he
"could recover if I shrieked
My heart's agony", '...but I am dumb
From human dignity'.

This is his only defence against 'the yelling pack' that he describes in the fourth poem.

    IV   The Death of the Hare

I have pointed out the yelling pack,
The hare leap to the wood,
And when I pass a compliment
Rejoice as lover should
At the drooping of an eye,
At the mantling of the bood.

Then suddenly my heart is wrung
By her distracted air
And I remember wildness lost
And after, swept from there,
Am set down standing in the wood
At the death of the hare.

The hare, or Lily, is a hunted, vulnerable creature, and the pack of hunting dogs (George, O'Higgins et al) finds its quarry at the end of the poem.

He avers that he has alerted the hare to the pack and to the safety of the wood (camouflage: costumes, make-up, changes of name and identity) but he remembers 'her distracted air'. Now he has been 'swept from there', is no longer in contact with her, and

'set down standing in the wood
At the death of the hare.'

This image is redolent of the corpse of Lily at the edge of the wood beside Ticknock crossroads. It seems that he warned his lover about those who would harm her, but she was caught anyway. The wood is a place of safety from the pack of hounds, but also of of mysterious darkness and secrecy.

In poem five he remembered unexpectedly finding Lily, her character, her body, "when all but dead of thirst" when he had forgotten about the existence of real love. has grieved until 'his beating heart would burst' since 'October last', but now, lonely and empty of grief, he is 'dry as bone'.

George inserted October in place of June to remove public suspicion of the involvement of the Yeats family and O'Higgins in Lily's death. 'June last' gives emphatic stress to the date, whereas 'October last' has no relevance, either in metre or in interpretation.

V   The Empty Cup

A crazy man that found a cup,
When all but dead of thirst,
Hardly dared to wet his mouth
Imagining, moon-accursed,
That another mouthful
And his beating heart would burst.
October last I found it too
But found it dry as bone,
And for that reason I am crazed
And my sleep is gone.

VI   His Memories

We should be hidden from their eyes,
Being but holy shows
And bodies broken like a thorn
Whereon the bleak north blows,
To think of buried Hector
And that none living knows.

The women take so little stock
In what I do or say
They'd sooner leave their cosseting
To hear a jackass bray;
My arms are like the twisted thorn
And yet there beauty lay;

The first of all the tribe lay there
And did such pleasure take –
She who had brought great Hector down
And put all Troy to wreck –
That she cried into this ear,
'Strike me if I shriek".

In the first verse of poem six he refers to himself and his wife as 'holy shows', that is as painted ceremonial statues of tortured saints, 'bodies broken like a thorn' in holy processions Whereon the bleak north [wind] blows.' His relationship with George has cooled in the wind of change, and they are both finding it difficult to keep face in public. He says he and George are like "buried Hector" of Greek mythology: like Hector they used to be an heroic couple, but they have now been publicly shamed, figuratively dragged on chariot wheels around an enemy's tomb, then slaughtered and buried.

This was of course symbolic, not real; details of how they were degraded were not made public: " ... none living knows"; in other words, the public is not aware of the facts of what happened, but all hold Yeats and his wife under suspicion of wrong-doing. This is why in the second verse he says women treat him like a jackass braying; they don't believe a word of what he says, no matter how loud he shouts. He remembers his joy at sleeping with Lily in the third verse:

"...the first of all the tribe lay there..." in his arms, before "She ... brought great Hector down / And put all Troy to wreck ... "

In Greek legend Aphrodite, the goddess of love, had promised her hero, Paris, that Helen would be his wife. She was the daughter of Zeus by either Leda or Nemesis and the most beautiful woman in the world. From among all her suitors she chose Menelaus as her husband. However during his absence Helen was wooed by Paris and fled to Troy with him, so that Menelaus declared war on Troy to reclaim his wife. Therefore Helen was the cause of the Trojan War. In poem X, "His Wildness" Yeats refers to himself as "Paris", the adulterer, and here he is referring to Lily as Helen. Menelaus is George, the wronged assassin. His use of this legend emphasises Yeats's desire to divorce his wife in order to marry Lily.

VII   The Friends of his Youth

Laughter not time destroyed my voice
And put that crack in it,
And when the moon's pot-bellied
I get a laughing fit,
For that old Madge comes down the lane,
A stone upon her breast,
And a cloak wrapped around the stone,

And she can get no rest
With singing hush and hush-a-bye;
She that has been wild
And barren as a breaking wave
Thinks that the stone's a child.

And Peter that had great affairs
And was a pushing man
Shrieks 'I am King of the Peacocks,'
And perches on a stone;
And then I laugh till tears run down
And the heart thumps at my side,
Remembering that her shriek was love
And that he shrieks from pride.

In the seventh poem, the "laughter" is not mirth: it is the uncontrollable humourless laughter of madness or extreme grief, of being unable to come to terms with reality. He "...gets a laughing fit ... when the moon's pot-bellied"; when the moon is full he thinks of Lily's pregnancy and of 'old Madge'.

In 1926 Margaret Magill was a widow of forty-eight with no children of her own, "...barren as a breaking wave..."

Once again Yeats is using Greek myth. Chronos, the Titan responsible for time, had many children by his wife Rhea; but her husband murdered each one at birth, as he knew they would overthrow him when older. Accordingly when Rhea next gave birth, she hid away her latest son, Zeus, pretending to be grieving with a stone under her shawl rather than a live child. When he saw her carrying a stone, Chronos would laugh hysterically. Meanwhile Zeus grew, eventually murdered his father and became King of the Gods. Yeats knows that Mrs McGill can never reveal his son; however he cannot control what the son may do when he is older.

VIII   Summer and Spring

We sat under an old thorn-tree
And talked away the night,
Told all that had been said or done
Since first we saw the light,
And when we talked of growing up
Knew that we'd halved a soul
And fell the one in t'other's arms
That we might make it whole;
Then Peter had a murdering look,
For it seemed that he and she
Had spoken of their childish days
Under that very tree.
O what a bursting out there was,
And what a blossoming,
When we had all the summer-time
And she had all the spring!

Poem eight, "Summer and Spring" describes two people falling in love in a rural or park location, probably St Stephen's Green. However it does not mention the seasons, so the title must refer to partners in the spring and summer of life, disparate in age. When Kevin was born Yeats was fifty-five and Lily was twenty. Nevertheless despite their thirty-five years age difference they had met their soulmates and began an affair;

"We knew we'd halved a soul
And fell the one in t'other's arms
That we might make it whole …"

In poem nine, Yeats sounds ashamed of his dealings with Lily,

Mrs McGill and Madge Hopkins.

IX   The Secrets of the Old

I have old women's secrets now
That had those of the young.
Madge tells me what I dared not think
When my blood was strong
And what had drowned a lover once
Sounds like an old song.

Though Margery is stricken dumb
If thrown in Madge's way,
We three make up a solitude
For none alive to-day
Can know the stories that we know
Or say the things we say:

How such a man pleased women most
Of all that are gone;
How such a pair loved many years
And such a pair but one,
Stories of the bed of straw
And the bed of down.

George has deliberately mixed up the names but they remain recognisable. Madge is Margaret McGill and Margery is Madge Hopkins[89]. Yeats begins by saying he has "... old women's secrets now, / That had those of the young." Lily had told Margaret who was the father of her child.

Mrs McGill obviously spoke her mind to Yeats, for she had told him "...what I dared not think / When my blood was strong..." criticising the relationship and its effect on Lily. She had an accusing look, for "...Margery is stricken dumb / If thrown in Madge's way..." Madge was blamed for contributing to Lily's death by bringing her to a meeting with Dillon; she was certainly blamed for withholding evidence in court.

Yeats says that all three share a secret about a love affair between different social classes, "...the bed of straw..." and the "...bed of down". He is also sure that they will never reveal the truth: "...We three make up a solitude: / For none alive today / Can know the stories that we know..."

X   His Wildness
O bid me mount and sail up there
Amid the cloudy wrack,
For Peg and Meg and Paris' love
That had so straight a back,
Are gone away, and some that stay
Have changed their silk for sack.

Were I but there and none to hear
I'd have a peacock cry,
For that is natural to a man
That lives in memory,
Being all alone I'd nurse a stone
And sing it lullaby.

Yeats is here wanting to die, to go 'up there Amid the cloudy wrack' because their honest love 'That had so straight a back' is 'gone away' and he is remorseful, changing his 'silk for sack'. He is now 'a man That lives in memory'.

If he were alone he would 'nurse a stone And sing it lullaby'. He is tormented by having had to abandon his son and would nurse him himself if he could. But to publicly recognise his son's foster-mother, location and identification would deliver him to Neligan's and O'Higgins forces, because George was watching his every move.

Yeats's poetry reveals his torment and culpability: from this point in his life, using Catholic symbolism, he expected purgatory when he died rather than heaven or hell. Heaven was for those who led a good life, and he could not claim that; Hell was for those who committed evil acts, the seven deadly sins, and he was not guilty of those.

But Purgatory, a place of cleansing, was for those who passively allowed evil to take place. Yeats felt guilty for passively allowing his wife to manipulate O'Higgins to murder Lily, destroying Kevin's, Madge's, Mrs McGill's, James's and his son's lives. From that amount of evil many would never recover. He was very estranged from George, and could no longer bear her presence, or that of her children for long. He realised that she was infinitely capable of evil.

XI   From Oedipus at Colonus

Endure what life God gives and ask no longer span;
Cease to remember the delights of youth, travel-wearied aged man;
Daylight becomes death-longing if all longing else be vain.

Even from that delight memory treasures so,
Death, despair, division of families, all entanglements of mankind grow,
As that old wandering beggar and these God-hated children know.

In the long echoing street the laughing dancers throng,
The bride is carried to the bridegroom's chamber through

torchlight and tumultuous song;
I celebrate the silent kiss that ends life short or long.

Never to have lived is best, ancient writers say;
Never to have drawn the breath of life, never to have looked into the eye of day;
The second best's a gay goodnight and quickly turn away.

The metre of this poem demonstrates despair and hopelessness; Yeats will simply 'Endure what life God gives' since Lily and their son are gone, so 'all longing else be vain'. He sees the destruction caused by his adultery to his legitimate family, whom he represents as 'that old wandering beggar and these God-hated children'. He regrets his life and is looking forward to death: 'a gay goodnight and quickly turn away'.

It is important to note that Yeats was seeing real changes in his public status, even though his wife and O'Higgins, via Neligan and O'Duffy, were very carefully guarding him from public disapprobation. The trial of Lily's alleged murderers had made public the corruption of the Minister of Justice, the Senate, the courts and administration and the whole Garda Siochana, and Yeats was suddenly seen as a man who had personal responsibility for the killing of his lover for his own benefit.

In his preface to "The Poems; W. B. Yeats", Daniel Albright writes of the derision that various writers felt for Yeats after 1925.

"The great poets of the next generation regarded him suspiciously."

For example Ezra Pound

"... turned increasingly hostile, dismissing 'The King of the

Great Clock Tower' with the single word 'Putrid'..." and "some of the later Cantos can be seen as a deliberate undoing of Yeats' creative work... For example Canto XCVI (1959) quotes genuine documents of Justinian's Constantinople ... setting forth the penalties for selling wine at false measure, or for building a wall that falls down ..."

Yeats felt that such degrading comments were justified in relation to his life, so he took no legal action against them. He was an honest man who understood people's feelings; if this had not been the case he could not have been successful as a poet, mage or politician.

He had been figuratively stuck between a stone and a hard place and was unable to budge after Lily had been murdered: should he abandon everything in his life for his illegitimate baby, who might be murdered; or should he abandon him to a relatively safe but poor and uncertain life, in order to secure his legitimate family, possessions and career?

In "Two Songs from a Play" written later, in 1931, he sees

"...a staring virgin stand" ... "And tear the heart out of his side
And lay the heart upon her hand
and bear that beating heart away."

He has lost his heart to this "fierce virgin", and the "Odour of blood" has destroyed all his work by making

"... all Platonic tolerance vain / And vain all Doric discipline."

He blames himself completely for this tragedy:

"Whatever flames upon the night
Man's own resinous heart has fed."

In 1942 T. S. Eliot wrote 'Little Gidding', in which an anguished spirit looking like Yeats comes on stage to say

Let me disclose the gifts reserved for age
To set a crown upon your lifetime's effort.
First, the cold friction of expiring sense
Without enchantment, ofering no promise
But bitter tastelessness of shadow fruit
As body and soul begin to fall asunder.
Second, the conscious impotence of rage
At human folly, and the laceration
Of laughter at what ceases to amuse.
And last, the rending pain of re-enactment
Of all that you have done, and been; the shame
Of motives late revealed...[90]

Albright continues:

"...in early drafts [T.S.] Eliot's anonymous ghost referred specifically to Yeats's political situation as well. [W.H.] Auden too evidently regarded Yeats as a monster looming behind his work.

...in a strange essay published in the year of Yeats's death, ' The Public vs. the Late Mr William Butler Yeats', Auden's 'Public Prosecutor' says, 'In 1900 he believed in fairies; that was bad enough; but in 1930 we are confronted with the pitiful, the deplorable spectacle of a grown man occupied with the mumbo-jumbo of magic[91] ...

And the protagonist of Auden's and [Chester] Kallman's libretto to Hans Werner Henze's 'Elegy For Young Lovers' is a wicked poet, clearly half-modelled on Yeats, who visits séances in order to be inspired, takes hormones to rejuvenate himself – and at last provokes the death of his mistress ... in order to stimulate interesting aesthetic emotions."[92]

After Lily's death Yeats's fame became infamy. By 1927 he had to give up his role in the Irish government; he became disillusioned with politics because he could not support communism or fascism, nationalism or unionism, war or tyranny.

He had to maintain the hypocritical public image of a happy family, but his wife became to him merely a personal secretary and child-minder.

He gave up all attempts to restrict her editing of his works, since she retained tight control of them in order to protect herself from public approbrium.

His children eventually grown up and moved away, thankful to visit him only on formal occasions. Long-standing friends like Maud faded away. All that Yeats had left was enough money to live out his years in the sunshine, indulging in substitute female friends, poetry and playwriting whilst waiting for Purgatory.

"Sailing to Byzantium" also written in 1925, describes his despair.

THAT is no country for old men.
The young in one another's arms, birds in the trees -
Those dying generations - at their song,
The salmon-falls, the mackerel-crowded seas,
Fish, flesh, or fowl, commend all summer long
Whatever is begotten, born, and dies.

Caught in that sensual music all neglect
Monuments of unageing intellect.

An aged man is but a paltry thing,
A tattered coat upon a stick, unless
Soul clap its hands and sing, and louder sing
For every tatter in its mortal dress,
Nor is there singing school but studying
Monuments of its own magnificence;
And therefore I have sailed the seas and come
To the holy city of Byzantium.

O sages standing in God's holy fire
As in the gold mosaic of a wall,
Come from the holy fire, perne in a gyre,
And be the singing-masters of my soul.
Consume my heart away, sick with desire
And fastened to a dying animal
It knows not what it is; and gather me
Into the artifice of eternity.

Once out of nature I shall never take
My bodily form from any natural thing,
But such a form as Grecian goldsmiths make
Of hammered gold and gold enamelling
To keep a drowsy Emperor awake;
Or set upon a golden bough to sing
To lords and ladies of Byzantium
Of what is past, or passing, or to come.

Yeats wishes to escape from the public world, become a beautiful bronze bird elevated above the world and observe it from an isolated vantage point. Events were happening fast and he was partly conducting them, partly ordering them to be done by others. He was far away from the common world on his own isolated perch of Senate, government, theatre and home.

During the next twelve months, as Kevin approached five years old, Yeats wrote about a visit to a convent primary school. The title shows his focus for this emotive poem: it is not a senator's visit, the nuns, or a primary school. He first sets the scene:

Among School Children

I walk through the long school-room questioning;
A kind old nun in a white hood replies
The children learn to cipher and to sing,
To study reading-books and history,
To cut and sew, be neat in everything
In the best modern way - the children's eyes
In momentary wonder stare upon
A sixty-year-old smiling public man.

He then pictures a scene one evening that revealed his complete affinity with Lily:

I dream of a Ledaean body, bent
Above a sinking fire, a tale that she
Told of a harsh reproof, or trivial event
That changed some childish day to tragedy –
Told, and it seemed that our two natures blent
Into a sphere from youthful sympathy,
Or else, to alter Plato's parable,
Into the yolk and white of the one shell.

Having recalled the depth of their relationship, he remembers her features and tries to find them in the children in front of him. But despite her beauty, her child is not to be seen:

And thinking of that fit of grief or rage
I look upon one child or t'other there
And wonder if she stood so at that age -
For even daughters of the swan can share
Something of every paddler's heritage -
And had that colour upon cheek or hair,
And thereupon my heart is driven wild:
She stands before me as a living child.

He is so moved by his mental image of her face and his son's possible resemblance to her that he is almost in tears. He struggles with his outward expression to make it acceptable to those around him:

Her present image floats into the mind -
Did Quattrocento finger fashion it
Hollow of cheek as though it drank the wind
And took a mess of shadows for its meat?
And I though never of Ledaean kind
Had pretty plumage once - enough of that,
Better to smile on all that smile, and show
There is a comfortable kind of old scarecrow.

Thinking about Lily, a young mother with her child, makes him remember his own mother. Would she be happy with the result of her labour sixty years later? Did a mother – Lily - think the trouble she had had in giving birth to a son was worthwhile? He remembers her tears at pregnancy and the childbirth:

What youthful mother, a shape upon her lap
Honey of generation had betrayed,
And that must sleep, shriek, struggle to escape
As recollection or the drug decide,

Would think her son, did she but see that shape
With sixty or more winters on his head,
A compensation for the pang of his birth,
Or the uncertainty of his setting forth?

How did youth mature into old age? How could one foresee what a baby would become?

Plato thought nature but a spume that plays
Upon a ghostly paradigm of things;
Solider Aristotle played the taws
Upon the bottom of a king of kings;
World-famous golden-thighed Pythagoras
Fingered upon a fiddle-stick or strings
What a star sang and careless muses heard:
Old clothes upon old sticks to scare a bird.

The nuns before him worship abstract images rather than flesh and blood. However Yeats assumes that statues and children both represent higher "...Presences". He calls out to this "...self-born mocker of man's enterprise", his son:[93]

Both nuns and mothers worship images,
But those the candles light are not as those
That animate a mother's reveries,
But keep a marble or a bronze repose.
And yet they too break hearts - O Presences
That passion, piety or affection knows,
And that all heavenly glory symbolise -
O self-born mockers of man's enterprise;

Each child's life is different from their parents' lives. The dance or blossoming of the individual does not have to mean physical harm, or destructive beauty leading to hardship in Lily's case, or long hours writing poems at night in his case:

Labour is blossoming or dancing where
The body is not bruised to pleasure soul,
Nor beauty born out of its own despair,
Nor blear-eyed wisdom out of midnight oil.

His son by Lily is like a chestnut tree, but which section? The leaf will last a season or lifetime, and wither away; the blossom will have an attractive life and produce seed for next season; but the bole or trunk will provide his future family line through generations.

O chestnut tree, great-rooted blossomer,
Are you the leaf, the blossom or the bole?

He ends with a heartrending question: how can we identify in the flesh the result of our passion? How can he identify his son with Lily?

O body swayed to music, O brightening glance,
How can we know the dancer from the dance?

Ruin, Wreck and Wrack

The last quoted poem shows clearly that Yeats did suffer emotionally from the absence of Lily and felt bereft at losing contact with Kevin. When Lily died he had not seen Kevin for at least two years; he had been warning her to take extra care because of his fear that his wife would murder Kevin, so he had deliberately avoided seeing him in his new covert life as Mrs McGill's son.[94]

On the day of the murder O'Higgins broke the news to Yeats and his wife; though George was jubilant, Yeats was very suddenly faced with his worst fear, judging by 'A Prayer to my Son'. Reeling with shock, he will have been required by O'Higgins, almost certainly accompanied by O'Duffy in his Commissioner role, to cover up preceding events in his own life. For O'Higgins, O'Duffy and also for Yeats as a senator, the British government must remain in ignorance of Yeats's affair with Lily. If Britain knew of the elderly stateman's affair with and illegitimate son by Lily and her subsequent murder by the Minister of Justice through manipulation of a serving police suerintendent and a peace commissioner, it would raise crucial doubts about the security of the Irish Free State, and control of the Irish government might have to be retained.

According to rumours that circulated behind closed doors after the trial Lily's son was common knowledge, and people said secretly that she was a spy. It is certain that she gave Yeats information about the "horrible green parrots" whom she saw, lived with and worked with every day, just as he certainly wanted to know about the Catholic working class and regularly donned camouflage to walk among them freely. These facts were probably what George told O'Higgins in order to convince him that Lily must be eliminated. However since Lily had never been a member of any political group, she probably did not have access to the type of information required by a spy. [95]

Yeats suffered socially. Olivia was confused about who had initiated this, so avoided the couple, leaving them to sort it out themselves. Oliver St John Gogarty expressed his disgust at their glib dishonesty when he saw what happened at the Abbey Theatre after the trial had ended. He soon left the Seanad. Edmund Dulac was disgusted at Yeats's actions; he stayed well away from his erstwhile friend. Maud Gonne wrote to him privately in her capacity as a Justice of the Peace for Sinn Fein:

"Go away into the sun & reflect on it, write poetry & pray to God to send men who understand what love of Ireland & of their fellows means to undo this mischief you - unwillingly perhaps - have helped to do. For your poetry you will be forgiven, but sin no more."[96]

No more honorary degrees were offered to him in Ireland, though he still got them from other countries where his problems were unknown. His political influence with English parliamentarians faded away.

The trial of Honor Bright's murderer ended on Friday, and the following Monday there was a riot at Yeats' Abbey Theatre about the first performance of Sean O'Casey's new play "The Plough and the Stars'. It featured a prostitute in the recently written Act II.

The trial of Honor Bright's murderers was still uppermost in the minds of the audience. People had been aware of Yeats' relationship with Lily; it had carried on for five or six years in the centre of town, and his disguise had probably slipped from time to time. Midwives, landlords, neighbours and passers-by might well have recognized him. Virtually all would have been lower class, of course, and in deference to authorities.

O'Casey knew Yeats well and had written a play to ridicule hypocrisy, pointless death and squandered lives. Rosie Redmond, the prostitute in the newly added Scene II, is the only character in the whole play that is not a hypocrite. He was openly deriding the Free State, as, in his socialist opinion, the working class had made no progress and was no better off than under British rule.

Joseph Holloway, a playwright and long-term supporter of the Abbey Theatre, wrote in his diary about the riots:

"Thursday February 4th [1926] ...Dublin is agog about [O'Casey's] new play.

Sunday February 7th I attended the dress rehearsal ... Act II [containing the new character of Rosie Redmond] is very badly managed ... Ria Mooney's part, a prostitute, in Act II is quite unnecessary...

Monday February 8th There was electricity in the air before and behind the curtain at the Abbey tonight when Sean O'Casey's play The Plough and the Stars was first produced. The theatre was thronged with distinguished people, and before the doors opened the queue to the pit entrance extended past old Abbey Street – not a quarter of them got in. The play was followed with feverish interest, and the players being called and recalled at the end of the piece. Loud calls for

"Author!" brought O'Casey on the stage, and he received an ovation.

Monty (James Montgomery, Irish Film Censor] said after Act II "I am glad I am off duty." ...The second Act carried realism to extremes...

F. R. Higgins, Liam O'Flaherty and others were in a group (of actors). (Politicians) Ernest Blythe and Mrs., the Lord Chief Justice and Mrs Kennedy, Kevin O'Higgins, Yeats and party steered into the Greenroom after Act II...

Tuesday February 9 The Abbey was again thronged ... Some four or five in the pit objected to the Volunteers [forerunners of the Irish Republican Army] bringing the flag into a pub in Act II. Kevin Barry's sister was one of the objectors. The pit door had to be shut to avoid a rush being made on it, and two policemen were on the scene. The audience relished the fight of the women in Act II and didn't object to the nasty incidents and phrases scattered here and there throughout the play ... Meeting Dr. Oliver Gogarty, Monty said, "I hope you are not going to say you liked it!" "I do," owned up Gogarty ... "It will give the smug-minded something to think about."

Thursday February 11 The protest of Tuesday night having no effect on the management, a great protest was made tonight, and ended in almost all the second act being played in dumb show, and pantomiming afterwards. People spoke from all parts of the house, and W. B. Yeats moved out from the stalls during the noise, and Kathleen O'Brennan ... told me Yeats went round to the Irish Times office to try to have the report of the row doctored. On his return to the theatre, he tried to get a hearing on the stage, but not a word he spoke could be heard.

... After Act I was the first I heard that a storm was brewing from Dan Breen ... Mrs. Pearse, Mrs Tom Clarke, Mrs Sheehy-Skeffington and others were in the theatre... Some of the players behaved with uncommon roughness to some ladies who got on the stage, and threw two of them into the stalls. One young man thrown from the stage got his side hurt by the piano. The chairs of the orchestra were thrown on the stage ... and some four or five tried to pull down half of the drop curtain...

... Mrs Sheehy-Skeffington from the back of the balcony during the din kept holding forth, and at the same time others were speaking in the pit: all were connected with Easter Week. A great big voice called "O'Casey out!" on "Rosie Redmond' appearing in Act II. Shouts of "Honor Bright" were heard.

Friday February 12 A detective-lined theatre presented itself at the beginning of the play tonight at the Abbey and there was no disturbance. ... None was allowed to stand in the passages to make way for the 'G' men, a body of men of evil fame in Ireland. ..."

The riot was initiated by the straight-talking play, but it was actually focussing on the injustice of what had happened to Honor Bright in the supposedly honourable Free State, and especially on Yeats's mendacity and treachery. Kevin Barry's sister, after whose brother Lily had named her son, was there too. Like Hannah Sheehy-Skeffington she was a noted upholder of justice and equality. O'Casey had written his play to show public distrust in the Free State, and the audience were giving him standing ovations because they had come to protest at Honor Bright's unpalatable killing and the tyrannical hypocrisy of the State in calling her a prostitute and acquitting her murderer.

Yeats was well protected by fellow politicians such as

O'Higgins, who were fully aware of the background to the riots, and by numerous police officers and detectives organised by the Chief Superintendent. They were in attendance for every performance of O'Casey's play; they knew that its timing would call out the masses who objected to the trial. Because of Neligan's presence the words 'Honor Bright' were avoided, since the Gardai would reward those who uttered them with at least an extra beating.

Newspapers were completely under the power of the state as can be seen by Yeats' reaction. First he told the audience from the stage that they were childish, and then he ran to the nearby newspaper office to dictate what he wanted them to write. He felt so threatened by the audience that he 'doctored' the newspaper report despite no one being able to hear him, so afraid was he that the truth of what people were saying would appear in writing.

Therefore none of the papers mentioned Honor Bright or her alleged murderer's trial despite widespread, overwhelming public unrest. Newspaper editors, the Ministry of Justice and the Garda acted together to suppress public disgust and dismay at their corruption. Critics were under the same constraints, declaring, "... the play and its women characters were worthy of derision and censorship...". It could not be said in public, but authorities, public and critics all linked Yeats inextricably to Honor Bright's fate. Evidently so did Gogarty, who considered O'Higgins, Yeats and fellow-politicians to be "smug-minded".

Countess Constance Markievicz did not attend the trial of Dillon and Purcell. Nor did she protest at O'Casey's "Plough and the Stars" at the Abbey Theatre. "Perhaps she deemed it better to remain silent on the subject of the play." She was in fact a close friend of O'Casey since they were both active nationalists who shared an interest in the Citizen's Army and related socialist ventures. She had also known Yeats since childhood, was very well informed about current affairs, and must have been profoundly depressed at the way the Free State had developed, and particularly about Yeats's conspiratorial machinations with O'Higgins. In 1925 she resigned as Chairperson of Cumann naMBan in order to support Eamon De Valera, thus showing her despair at Free State nationalism by moving to republicanism.

Dr Purcell, no longer a Peace Commissioner, returned to his surgery as a GP after acquittal, but realised that his list of patients was dwindling to nothing. When his wife went shopping in Blessington she was very distraught at repeatedly being refused service. They soon relocated to Kent in England, where Dr Purcell joined another practice. His son of the same name also became a doctor.

Leo Dillon had been sacked from the Garda, so on acquittal he had no job to go to. It soon became apparent that he would not get another in Ireland and that his life was in danger, so he returned without delay to his parents in Wales. On 1st April he emigrated from Liverpool to St John, New Brunswick, Canada, on the 'Montclare' (Canadian Pacific Railway Line) arriving on 10th April 1926. His father had paid his fare. He declared himself a 'farmer' and gave his address as 17 Clare Street, Cardiff. Later he married Isabel Margaret Jean Brown, the daughter of Harry W. Brown and Helen Edy and they had children. He lived quietly as a farmer for the rest of his life. His descendants only discovered his murky Irish past in late 2014 whilst researching family genealogy.[97]

On Sunday 10th July 1927 Kevin O'Higgins[98] was shot dead as he left home at Cross Avenue, Booterstown, Dublin on his way to mass at the Church of the Assumption. Three well-known Anti-Treaty IRA men, Timothy Coughlin, Bill Gannon and Archie Doyle, executed him but were not arrested. A Garda informer murdered Coughlin in 1928, while Gannon and Doyle were given an amnesty by de Valera when he created a republic in 1932. The motive for his murder was never explored since there were a thousand motives, including Honor Bright.

Commissioner O'Duffy held his post until Eamon de Valera dismissed him in February 1933. He then became active in the fascist movement, was given command of the Army Comrades Association, known as Blueshirts, and renamed it the 'National Guard' with marches, flags, salutes ('Hail O'Duffy') based on Hitler's Nazi regime. National Guard and left-wing groups fought in the streets. In August 1933 the government banned the National Guard from marching to Leinster Lawn in Dublin. The following month O'Duffy helped establish the Fine Gael Party, becoming president, and causing considerable controversy by describing the Irish Republican Army as communist. In August the following year he was forced to resign.

Olivia Shakespear distanced herself initially, but after two years she wrote to Yeats again as a friend.

Ezra Pound invited Yeats and George to Rapallo in Italy because Dorothy was a close friend of George. He began to write swingeing criticism of Yeats and stopped trying to emulate his poetry. He took on a mistress to whom he became devoted, and they raised an illegitimate daughter. He and Dorothy had no children. After the Second World War he was accused of fascism by America and sent to a mental home. He met George again in 1965; by this time she was a terminal alcoholic.

When Kevin was four he remembered having a bath in front of the fire and having his hair and nails cut. Afterwards he put on new clothes including socks and shoes; he had never worn them before. Then his mother, Mrs McGill, took him across town to a big house with lots of well-dressed people in it. He was asked many questions. Afterwards the two of them walked home. As a four-year-old he had no idea who these people were. However he may unknowingly have witnessed his foster mother being strongly advised by Neligan to keep silent about what she knew.

From that date Mrs McGill received no more fees to keep Kevin. Nevertheless she continued to look after him and treating him as her own son, raising him with maternal care and integrity. She, Kevin, her partner James White and his son carried on living in the one-room cellar of 2 Catherine Street with a dirt floor, fireplace, table, two dining chairs and a straw mattress in the corner. They had sugar or potato sacks as bedsheets with ex-army blankets above, and when it was cold they used their coats. The water tap and shared earth closets were out in the yard.

Kevin really loved his father, the nicest, kindest man in the world. James White had fought in the Great War but died when he was nine around 1929-30. His mother "taught him right from wrong"[99]. She never had any money so she took in washing, but things improved when his brother left school a few years later at 14 and became a delivery boy. As well as earning money he got a free uniform and bicycle. Kevin also left school at 14 despite being good at his studies; the Christian Brothers urged his mother to let him stay on, but she couldn't; there wasn't enough money to pay for it. Kevin was intensely disappointed; he wanted to study more than anything else in life.

In 1942 aged twenty-one Kevin enlisted in the British Army to escape from unskilled labour in Ireland. To prove his age he required a birth certificate. It stated that he was the illegitimate son of Lily O'Neill – a prostitute people still talked about - who had been murdered when he was four years old. No father was named; he had no living relatives. He did intend to return to Ireland to find out about his parents, but raising his own family always took precedence. He died of a heart attack in 1980 aged 59.

Nothing is known of what happened to Madge Hopkins. Few options remain available for a single woman accused of fornication and prostitution and blackmailed by the police. As she had no prospects of marriage or a job, prostitution, madness or suicide are possibilities. If she was lucky she emigrated.

Yeats wrote 'Byzantium' in 1930. There is a contrasting image in 'Sailing to Byzantium' written in 1925.

The unpurged images of day recede;
The Emperor's drunken soldiery are abed;
Night resonance recedes, nightwalkers' song
After great cathedral gong;
A starlit or a moonlit dome disdains
All that man is,
All mere complexities,
The fury and the mire of human veins.
Before me floats an image, man or shade,
Shade more than man, more image than a shade;
For Hades' bobbin bound in mummy-cloth
May unwind the winding path;
A mouth that has no moisture and no breath
Breathless mouths may summon;
I hail the superhuman;

I call it death-in-life and life-in-death.
Miracle, bird or golden handiwork,
More miracle than bird or handiwork,
Planted on the star-lit golden bough,
Can like the cocks of Hades crow,
Or, by the moon embittered, scorn aloud In glory of changeless metal
Common bird or petal
And all complexities of mire or blood.
At midnight on the Emperor's pavement flit
Flames that no faggot feeds, nor steel has lit,
Nor storm disturbs, flames begotten of flame,
Where blood-begotten spirits come
And all complexities of fury leave,
Dying into a dance,
An agony of trance,
An agony of flame that cannot singe a sleeve.
Astraddle on the dolphins' mire and blood,
Spirit after Spirit!
The smithies break the flood.
The golden smithies of the Emperor!
Marbles of the dancing floor
Break bitter furies of complexity,
Those images that yet
Fresh images beget,
That dolphin-torn, that gong-tormented sea.

The poet has somehow moved from "sages standing in God's holy fire" in the first poem, to a courtyard filled with "blood-begotten spirits" in the second. He has been transformed into an ethereal observer in the city. He is not having any impact on his world and cannot introduce any order into it. The Emperor of Byzantium is out of sight, and his agents are out of line and impotent ('the Emperor's drunken soldiery are abed'). Who holds power in this world? Lily O'Neill is the 'shade', the 'blood-begotten spirit', or bird in stanza 3 that he is referring to. He imagines her anger and grief.

At Algeciras – A Meditation upon Death

The heron-billed pale cattle-birds
That feed on some foul parasite
Of the Moroccan flocks and herds
Cross the narrow Straits to light
In the rich midnight of the garden trees
Till the dawn break upon those mingled seas.

Often at evening when a boy
Would I carry to a friend -
Hoping more substantial joy
Did an older mind commend –
Not such as are in Newton's metaphor,
But actual shells of Rosses' level shore.

Greater glory in the sun,
An evening chill upon the air,
Bid imagination run
Much on the great questioner;
What can he question, what if questioned I
Can with a fitting confidence reply.

Written November 1928

By 1928 he has realised that other people hold him responsible, that he is merely a human being. Hence his depression from which there can be no escape. He still believes in a fundamental God, so from this point onwards his poems reveal despair and an expectation of Purgatory, an enforced cleansing of his soul after death. He also knows that his erstwhile social life is finished, as senator, poet, playwright, theatre manager, politician or lover. Even as a husband and father he cannot function properly any more.

'Legendary' Honor Bright

Was Lily a prostitute, as some Dubliners insist?

Although I never knew my grandmother, I would say not; my father was not touched by the mental and physical distress that a prostitute would have felt in Dublin in 1925. Mrs McGill was paid regularly until his mother died, though this would have been very difficult for a woman with a highly irregular income. Her charge was always well fed, properly brought up and well educated, despite financial hardship.

Kevin had great concentration, was always reading and always collected books, glass, coins and stamps. He rarely drank alcohol, and was kind and altruistic with a great sense of social justice and fairness, running a local trade union for many years and keen to help those less fortunate than himself. These characteristics do not strike me as emerging from a disorganised upbringing.

Nevertheless stories of Lily being a prostitute persist. Many are in articles or books written forty-five years or more after her murder, not earlier because of the absolute Garda ban on all references to her in the press after 1926.

This ban was abandoned in 1971 when the Dublin Evening Herald printed a series of articles based on a letter received from Esther Kennedy. A Dublin resident aged 78, Esther still lived in the Dublin convent where she had worked as a laundress; in other words she had been a prostitute and an unmarried mother some decades before. She died shortly after writing the letter.

Esther said:"I knew Honor Bright in her early days as a street-walker. This was after the birth of her child, a boy, born in the Coombe Hospital on November 1st, 1920 [sic] – the day that Kevin Barry was hanged in Mountjoy.

"With twenty-five other girls of 'the unfortunate class' we lived in a lodging house at 25 Chancery Lane, off Golden Lane.[sic] The house is now gone. Honor was just an ordinary girl, stocky in build, not particularly good-looking, with dark bobbed hair framing a plain face. She was not a rough type.[sic]

"She seldom drank. Some of us used to drink methylated spirits, which had a kick in it. Honor used to buy Hall's wine.

"When the house in Chancery Lane was closed through the efforts of Frank Duff and others in the Legion of Mary we, meaning the street-walkers, were taken first to Baldoyle Retreat House and then to a hostel in Harcourt Street, run by the Legion.

"Honor refused to come with us to Baldoyle or Harcourt Street, as she would not part with her child, whom she loved dearly and for whom she paid £1 a week every Sunday morning to a single woman, who was in effect his foster-mother.[sic]

"From Chancery Lane Honor went to live in Newmarket, No 48, with a few other girls who also did not want to go to Baldoyle.[sic] Some time later the lodging house in Chancery Lane was re-opened and some of us went back there.

"On June 9th, 1925 while then in the hostel in Harcourt Street, we read in the papers of the murder of a girl at Ticknock, and from the description we assumed that the girl must be Honor Bright.

"That nightsome of us made our way from Harcourt Street – it being our evening off – to the Lamb Doyle's pub in the mountains, to see the body.

"I overheard one of the girls in our party whom we knew as Margaret Walshe (but it wasn't her real name) say "I told Honor not to go in that car."[sic] I am convinced Margaret was the girl who earlier in the night stole the money and the cigarette case from the doctor.

"Later, on the fatal night, this girl, who also lived with Honor in the lodging house in Newmarket, persuaded Honor to swap clothes with her, and gave Honor her own worn grey costume to put on.[sic]

"Honor was a poor slob of a girl.[sic] She went in that grey costume to Stephen's Green and was murdered in it. She was a harmless girl who never stooped to theft.

"That girl who made the swap was a real adventuress. She had the 'signature' of many prominent people and was well got on all sides. She was not called on to give evidence, and there was no mention during the trial of the swap. After the trial that girl was despatched to Canada, where she remained for five years.

"Honor never spoke about her relatives or discussed where she came from, although we knew it was from County Carlow. It was a cruel death for such an inoffensive girl. God rest her soul. The rosary beads found on her body were given to her by a Franciscan."

Most of the true facts Esther mentions were from newspaper accounts of the investigation and trial, written by journalists. One true fact, the birth of Honor's son (though the date is wrong), is from someone who knew about her. However Dublin was then a small city, so anyone could have been the source of rumours after the trial. In any case, the court insistence that Honor was a prostitute made real prostitutes, often women with learning dificulties, imagine themselves working alongside her. Zanzibar Films, who attempted to make a film about her in 2008 but had not researched her adequately, also asserted that Honor Bright had a son.

Honor is never called by any other name by Esther, although in reality fellow lodgers knew her as 'Lizzie' O'Neill. Esther was a prostitute living in a brothel in Chancery Lane, whereas in fact Lily always lived in Catherine Street from 1920 to 1922, then in Newmarket, as a shop assistant, next to a police station until her death.

Esther is also wrong about the identity of Bridie, whose given name was Madge Hopkins, not Margaret Walshe. Esther does not mention her being interviewed by the police. The obvious absence of some of Madge's evidence during the trial was the trigger for rumourmongers to fill gaps. Here Esther says Bridie was not called forward; in fact she did give limited evidence. The most important witness not called forward was in fact Mrs McGill.

The police photographs in this book show that Honor was wearing her own clothes and they were well fitting and relatively new; however the photos were never available to the general public until now, so stories about Honor's clothing and appearance have been made up at will.

Esther implies that Honor had a violent death, but the photos show that Lily was not molested apart from the bullet.

Yeats's lover,

'Leda', 'a proud woman', 'the first of all the tribe'

was also a completely different character to the one described by Esther

'a poor slob of a girl ... a harmless girl who never stooped to theft.

Esther Kennedy had lived all of her adult life in brothels or convents along with other women of her own age, and they were all encouraged to weave myths about Honor when she became notorious as a prostitute, thanks to political chicanery.

Moreover Esther's letter was an attempt by Kevin O'Connor, the journalist who wrote for her as she was illiterate, to revive erotic memories of his readership and increase sales of his newspaper. No doubt Esther, as an ailing old woman, received appropriate compensation. In 1995 O'Connor recycled Esther's story in the chapter headed 'The Cruel End of Honour Bright' in his book 'Thou Shalt Not Kill: True-life Stories of Irish Murders'.

León Ó Broin wrote Frank Duff's biography in 1972 after Duff died. A civil servant working at the Land Commission, from 1913 Duff became an ardently religious Catholic, and regularly visited the poor. By 1918 he was president of St Patrick's Conference in Myra House, Francis Street, not far from Newmarket where Honor lived. In 1921 he was "the essential founder member"[100] of the Legion of Mary, giving practical aid to women who needed it. In 1925, wanting to demonstrate his pride in the new Free State and destroy the corruption the British had instituted in Dublin, he organised a group of Catholic women to clear the street of prostitutes. They worked around his Francis Street headquarters, rather than in the Monto[101]. Therefore they heard all the rumours about Honor Bright. One of these women was Emmy Colgan. According to Duff's biographer

"...Lynch's at 48 Newmarket was the other lodging house Emmy got to know. It was packed with 'street girls', among them a refined girl who passed as 'Honour Bright'. She had served her time at Switzer's, never used bad language, and was, Emmy said, 'a lovely person to talk to'. She had not been going to Mass, but promised to go 'next Sunday'. 'Maybe' said her companion Bridie Foran, 'you mightn't be alive next Sunday.' Nor was she. She was found dead on Dublin mountains, murdered."

There is no way of knowing who originally told it, but the biography attributes this story to Emmy, not to Duff.

Switzer's was a ladies' dress shop in Dublin city centre and may have been where Lily worked, but there is no evidence to confirm this. Emmy tells us that Lynch's lodging, where Lily and Madge lived, was a brothel. Emmy says it was 'packed with street girls'; this is not how it is described by the three other residents, the landlady and her son in the witness depositions made prior to the alleged murderers' trial.

Emmy does not know about the police station next door. However her story does reflect what the prosecutor said in court and what newspapers reported. Like Esther she is mistaken about the identity of 'Bridie' and gives her a different name. She says that Honor Bright was 'refined', not realising that Lily came from a poor Carlow family.

Collette Gill, 'a sprightly old lady'[102] in 1972, from the same Legion of Mary group

"... added a detail to the story of 'Honour Bright'. She found her in the lodging house sharing a bed with another girl, lying on her back with her knees up. The following week [Honor] was apparently a resident in Sancta Maria when news of her murder filled the newspapers. Sarsfield Hogan, who then worked alongside Frank in the Department of Finance, questioned him about it. Frank told him that the unfortunate girl had left the hostel on that Saturday night in early spring, and that he had gone out looking for her, hoping to be able to persuade her to return to the hostel. He had found her sitting swinging herself on the chains which then lined the footpaths around St Stephen's Green. She was opposite the Shelbourne Hotel where there was great activity following some big sporting event, and a chance of 'custom'. Frank pleaded with her, and she had said to him "I'll come back tomorrow. I promise I will, Mr Duff. Honour bright."

Once again Collette is relating her addition to that told by another member of her group; they are unconsciously weaving a story together. Once again this tale is told nearly 50 years after the death of Duff, and without his sanction. Once again the witness depositions differ; in this story before her demise Honor moves into a hostel, a less permanent address, and shares a bed with another girl, lewdly lying on her back with her knees up in front of the others.

Details stated in court and echoed in newspapers, such as Honor swinging on the park chains opposite the hotel, are included as tokens of veracity by the teller. In this story Lily died on Saturday night, though in real life it was Tuesday night. Once again Lily's actual co-lodgers called her 'Lizzie', though Collette does not know her by that name.

Other details were added to the story wherever possible. For example,

" Dossiers were kept on all the girls, and ...there was one sad item ... Was this Honour Bright? Her file recorded that she had returned to her old ways, and in January 1933, when 'not in the Hostel, she had lost her life in tragic circumstances'.[103]

One regrets this sad demise, but this prostitute had nothing to do with Honor Bright because January 1933 was eight years after Lily's murder. Her ghost 'return[ing] to her old ways' had entered the public mind however; it is echoed in the song "Honor Bright" written in 1975 by Peter Yeates, performed with his band 'Full Shilling', in which Honor haunts Merrion Row in Dublin, where Yeats used to live.

Such stories as these were still regularly told in 2008 when I began to ask Dubliners about her. Men, who remembered the Garda insisting that she was the greatest prostitute Dublin had ever known, retold underground rumours with erotic relish.

But nobody could give me any actual evidence for these fantasies. Nobody had realised that the Garda "G" division had whitewashed history, inventing the myth to deflect attention from Yeats for being in love with her and giving her a son, and from George Yeats, Kevin O'Higgins and Leo Dillon for murdering her.

Neligan's efforts to cover up Lily's actual identity for the working class were aided by George Yeats's meticulous efforts for the literary world. She had taken to co-writing her husband's poetry on marriage, although he had written poetry about Lily on his own. However she was always very careful to keep knowledge of his affair away from the public eye; that was a talent she had learnt from her parents who had plenty of experience of her situation.

She increased her efforts from 1925, afraid of being accused of instigating Lily's murder; every word produced by Yeats was checked over to eliminate references to Lily or her child; names, dates of writing, sequence and even places were changed to remove suspicion of involvement. She also insisted on publicity showing the Yeats as a serenely happy family, although this became harder to maintain as the years rolled on.

After Yeats's death she took all his papers into her possession and became well known for hoarding and parsimony. She gave out papers only to those whom she knew would follow her required interpretation of her husband's life. She created a myth that Yeats, despite his penurious upbringing, was a refined upper class poet and politician with no sympathy for or understanding of Catholicism or the lower class, and refuted every interpretation of his 'masks'.

The journalist who wrote the most famous (or infamous) book, 'Honor Bright: the Full Story of a Famous Dublin Murder' combining it with 'Nighttown: The Story of Monto, Dublin's Notorious Red-Light District' was John Finegan. Dublin journalists view this book as the Bible in regard to Honor Bright.

Published in 1995, it is dedicated to a young Evening Mail reporter who covered the whole story "from Day One", while the acknowledgements show that it is exclusively taken from what was printed in Dublin newspapers.

Finegan's first paragraph sets the tone: "There are few who have not heard the now legendary name..." [Honor Bright] as it "... reverberates down the years in the memory of generations of Dubliners."[104]

Finegan tells us that "legendary" Honor's name is Elizabeth O'Neill, daughter of a prosperous farmer in County Carlow.

Elizabeth O'Neill was the name chosen by journalists on the Evening Mail in 1925. As I found out decades later, there are no entries in 1900 in the Irish register of births for Lily O'Neill or Honor Bright. The nearest name reporters could find was Elizabeth, so they wrongly assumed that Lizzie was an abbreviation (though it was chosen for sounding like Lily).

Finegan freely added other assumptions to this, e.g. 'She had a good education,' [105] and 'As a child she was known as Lil.'[106] He states that from 1919 'Lil' served 'an apprenticeship at Gorevan's drapery store in Lower Camden Street ... lived over the shop and had ... meals provided on the premises,' and she had 'deep brown eyes', which is strange since none of my family have eyes that colour. Finegan states, again with no evidence, that she became 'almost a nightly patron of the [dance] halls on the south side of the city. Often she danced the whole night through...'[107]

He says Honor 'dared not go home to her father and stepmother', not realising that she had no living parents and that her father never remarried. He echoed the 1971 newspaper article by Esther Kennedy, saying that 'she found frugal lodgings in Chancery Lane ...' and her son 'was born on November 1, 1920...' After the birth he says she became 'a late-night street-walker' or 'in the term universally in vogue in conversation at the time', 'a member of the unfortunate class'.'

He freely quotes from Esther's words written by Kevin O'Connor, that she used 'Honor Bright' '...frequently ... in conversation with a client on the street as a mark of reliability', that she ' ... paid a single woman £1 a week to care for her young son ... and called regularly to see him', that she had been living in Chancery Lane and refused to transfer to Harcourt Street, and that 'In 1923-24 she moved ... to Newmarket...' and '...shared a room with another street-walker...'

Finegan embellished this fabricated account with his own invention: 'Honor's usual beat as a street-walker was from Grafton Street to St Stephen's Green.' Until he wrote this in 1995 no one had ever mentioned or fabricated a beat, clients or income for Lily's fictitious occupation - not even the court.

Using the perjury proclaimed in the illegal, unjust trial and recorded in contemporary newspapers, he had conjured up new fairy-tales about "legendary" Honor Bright. Members of the Garda and the judiciary in Ireland still ardently defend these unsubstantial stories, being anxious to wash their hands of previous misdeeds and corruption.

But at last, after ninety years, the truth is out.

Bibliography

Albright, Daniel (1972) *The Myth Against Myth: A Study of Yeats's Imagination in Old Age,* Oxford University Press

Albright, Daniel ed. (1990 updated 1994) *Everyman: The Poems, W. B. Yeats*, London, J. M. Dent

Alldritt, Keith (1997) *W. B. Yeats: The Man and the Milieu* London John Murray

Arrington, Lauren (2010) *W. B. Yeats, The Abbey Theatre, Censorship, and The Irish State:*

Adding the Half-Pence to the Pence Oxford, Oxford University Press

Auden, W. H. and Kallman, Chester (1961) *Elegy For Young Lovers: Opera in three acts*. Mainz, B Schott's Soehne

Behan, Brendan (1974) *Richard's Cork Leg* New York, Grove Press Inc.

Bradford, Curtis (1970) *Reflections by W. B. Yeats transcribed and edited from the Journals* Dublin, The Cuala Press

Bradford, Curtis B. (1977) *W. B. Yeats – The Writing of The Player Queen* Northern Illinois University Press

Bradford, Curtis B. (1978) *Yeats at Work (Abridged)* New York, The Ecco Press

Bradley, Anthony (2011) *Imagining Ireland in the Poems and Plays of W. B. Yeats, Nation, Class and State* Palgrave Macmillan

Brown, Terence (2001) *The Life of W. B. Yeats* Dublin, Gill & Macmillan

Clifford, Brendan (2007) *Fianna Fáil and the Decline of the Free State.* Cork Ireland, Aubane Historical Society

Collins, Michael (1996) *The Path to Freedom* Welsh Academic Press

Coogan, Tim Pat (1991) *Michael Collins* Arrow Books

Cowell, Raymond (1969) *Literature in Perspective: W. B. Yeats*. London, Evan Brothers Limited

Cullingford, Elizabeth ed. (1984) **Yeats: Poems, 1919-1935: A Selection of Critical Essays.** London, Macmillan

Ellis-Fermor, Una (1939 reprinted 1977) *The Irish Dramatic Movement* London, Methuen & Co. Ltd.

Ellmann, Richard (1986) *Four Dubliners* Cardinal Sphere Books Limited

Ellmann, Richard (1987) *Yeats: The Man and The Masks*. Penguin Books

Fanning, Ronan (2013) **Fatal Path: British Government and Irish Revolution 1910-1922.** London, Faber and Faber

Ferriter, Diarmaid (2005) *The Transformation of Ireland 1900-2000* London, Profile Books

Finegan, John (1995) *Honor Bright: The Full Story of a Famous Dublin Murder and Nighttown: The Story of Monto, Dublin's Notorious Red-Light District* Dublin, Elo Publications

Foster, R. F. (2001) *The Irish Story: Telling Tales and Making It Up In Ireland.* London, Allen Lane The Penguin Press

Foster, R. F. (2003) *W. B. Yeats: A Life. II: The Arch-Poet*. London, Oxford University Press

Foy, Michael T. (2008) *Michael Collin's Intelligence War: The Struggle between the British and the IRA 1919-1921* Stroud, The History Press

Gogarty, Oliver St John (1954) *As I Was Going Down Sackville Street* Penguin Books

Gogarty, Oliver St John (1982) *Tumbling in the Hay* London, Sphere Books Ltd.

Graf, Susan Johnston (2000) *W. B. Yeats: Twentieth Century Magus* Maine, Samuel Weiser Inc.

Harper, Margaret Mills (Spring 2002) *Nemo: George Yeats and her Automatic Script* New Literary History, Vol 33, No. 2 Anonymity

Hazlehurst, Elizabeth C. (2012) *O'Casey's Women* Nottingham, Russell Press

Heaney, Seamus (2000) *Selected poems by W. B. Yeats* London, Faber and Faber

Howes, Marjorie and Kelly, John ed. (2006 reprinted 2008) *The Cambridge Companion to W. B. Yeats* Cambridge, Cambridge University Press

Hughes, Patricia (2014) *An Analysis of Selected Poetry by William Butler Yeats between 1918 and 1928* Hues Books

Inglis, Brian (No date; circa 1960?) *The Story of Ireland* London, Faber and Faber

Jeffares, A. Norman (1990) *W. B. Yeats: A New Biography*. Arena, Random Century Group

Jeffares, Norman and MacBride White, Anna ed. (1994) *Maud Gonne MacBride: A Servant of the Queen* Gerrards Cross, Colin Smythe

Jordan, Anthony J. (2003) *W. B. Yeats: Vain, Glorious, Lout: A Maker of Modern Ireland* Dublin, Westport Books

Kearns, Kevin C. (1994) *Dublin Tenement Life: An Oral History* Dublin, Gill and Macmillan

Kermode, Frank; White, John; Hawcroft, Francis (1961) *Images of a Poet: W. B. Yeats* University of Manchester, Whitworth Art Gallery

Krimm, Bernard G. (1981) *W. B. Yeats and the Emergence of the Irish Free State: 1918-1939: Living in the Explosion* New York, Whitston Publishing Company Inc.

Lambirth, Andrew (1999) *W. B. Yeats: A Biography with Selected Poems* London, Brockhampton Press

Londraville, Janis and Richard (1999) *Too Long A Sacrifice: The Letters of Maud Gonne and John Quinn* Associated University Presses, Inc.

Longenbach, James (1988) *Stone Cottage: Pound, Yeats & Modernism* Oxford, Oxford University Press

Lowery, Robert G. ed. (1984) *A Whirlwind in Dublin: The Plough and the*

Stars Riots. Connecticut, Greenwood Press

Luddy, Maria (2007) *Prostitution and Irish Society 1800-1940* Cambridge University Press

Mac Liammóir, Micheál, Boland, Eavan (1971) *W. B. Yeats* London Thames and Hudson

MacBride White, Anna and Jeffares, A. Norman ed. (1993) *The Gonne – Yeats Letters 1893 – 1938* New York W. W. Norton & Company

Macrae, Alasdair D. F. (1995) *W. B. Yeats: A Literary Life* London, Macmillan

Maddox, Brenda (1999) *George's Ghosts: A New Life of W. B. Yeats*. London, Picador

Maddox, Brenda (1999) *Yeats's Ghosts [The Secret Life of W. B. Yeats]* New York, HarperCollins Publishers

Makin, Peter (1992) *Pound's Cantos* Baltimore, The John Hopkins University Press

Martin, Augustine (1992) *Yeats: Collected Poems* London, Vintage Books

McCormack, (2005) W. J. *Blood Kindred: W. B. Yeats: The Life, The Death, The Politics* London, Pimlico

McInerney, Sarah (2008) *Where No One Can Hear You Scream: Murder and Assault in the Wicklow Mountains* Dublin, Gill and Macmillan

Murray, Christopher **Sean O'Casey: The Plough and the Stars: Educational Edition with notes for students** (2000) London, Faber& Faber Ltd.

Murray, Patrick (2000) *Oracles of God: The Roman Catholic Church and Irish Politics 1922-37* Dublin, University College Dublin Press

Neligan, David (1968) *The Spy in the Castle* London, Prendeville Publishing Limited

Ó Broin, León (1982) *Frank Duff: A Biography* Dublin, Gill and Macmillan

O'Casey Sean (1949) **Autobiography Book 4: Inishfallen Fare Thee Well.**

London, Pan Books Ltd.

O'Casey, Sean (1926) *Two Plays.* London, Macmillan & Co., Limited

O'Casey, Sean, writing as P.O. Cathasaigh (2003) *The Story of the Irish Citizen Army*. Hawaii, University Press of the Pacific, Honolulu

O'Connor, Garry (1989) *Sean O'Casey: A Life*. London, Paladin Books Collins Publishing Group

O'Connor, Kevin (1995) *Thou Shalt Not Kill: True-life Stories of Irish Murders* Dublin, Gill and Macmillan

O'Connor, Ulick (1975) *The Troubles: The Struggle for Irish Freedom 1912-1922* London, Mandarin, Octopus Publishing Group

Patel, Rajeshwari (1990) *W. B. Yeats* New Delhi, Prestige Books in association with Indian Society for Commonwealth Studies

Pearce, Donald R. (2001) *The Senate Speeches of W. B. Yeats* London Prendeville Publishing Limited

Pogson, Rex (1952) *Miss Horniman and the Gaiety Theatre Manchester* London, Rockliff Publishing Corporation Ltd.

Porter, Peter Selected by (1990) *W. B. Yeats: The Last Romantic* London, Aurum Press

Rattigan, Cliona (2012) *What Else Could I Do? Single Mothers and Infanticide, Ireland 1900-1950* Dublin, Irish Academic Press

Regan. John M. (2013) *Myth and the Irish State* Irish Academic Press

Saddlemyer, Ann (2002) *Becoming George: The Life of Mrs W. B. Yeats.* New York, Oxford University Press

Shaw, George Bernard (1932 reprinted 1933) *St Joan, The Apple Cart* London, Constable and Company Limited

Stallworthy, Jon ed. (1968 reprinted 1975) *Yeats: Last Poems: A Selection of Critical Essays* London, Casebook Series, The Macmillan Press

Tuohy, Frank (1976) *Yeats An Illustrated Biography* New York, New Amsterdam

Wade, Allen, ed. (1955) **The Letters of W B Yeats** London, Macmillan

Wordsworth Poetry Library, (1994) **The Collected Poems of W. B. Yeats** Wordsworth Editions Limited

Yeats, W. B. (1893) **The Poems of William Blake** London, Lawrence & Bullen

Yeats, W. B. (1934, reprinted 1977) **The Collected Plays of W. B. Yeats.** London, Macmillan

Yeats, W. B. (1965) **The Autobiography of William Butler Yeats consisting of Reveries over Childhood and Youth, The Trembling of the Veil and Dramatis Personae** New York, Macmillan Publishing Company

Yeats, W. B., Chosen by (1936, reprinted 1941) **The Oxford Book of Modern Verse 1892-1935.** Oxford, Clarendon Press

Notes

[1] Now Dun Laoghaire.
[2] Hone p. 185
[3] This quote is from a blog on www.TheWildGeese.Irish by Lisa Fortin Jackson on Feb. 4th 2014.
[4] Hone p. 231
[5] The Hibernian Club for politicians.
[6] Keith Alldritt, *The Man and the Milieu* p. 215
[7] Hone p. 301
[8] A. Norman Jeffares. W B Yeats: *A New Biography* p. 155
[9] Curtis Bradford *Reflections* p. 3
[10] As Ezra calls him.
[11] Yeats saw himself as British while de Valera was a committed Republican.

[12] Until the Second World War Irish people travelling to America did not need passports.
[13] Hone pp. 281-2
[14] *Becoming George: The Life of Mrs W B Yeats* by Ann Saddlemyer 2002 OUP. All facts in this chapter are taken from this book except where otherwise stated.

[15] In 1870 the first Married Women's' Property Act had given married women possession of their own earnings. The second Act of 1882 gave married women the same rights over their property as unmarried women, so that goods and chattels owned before marriage, such as clothing, jewellery, land and houses, would no longer belong to a husband after the wedding day. The third Act of 1893 gave married women full control over any kind of property acquired during marriage, even inheritance.
[16] In 1937 Yeats published a new version of 'The Vision' written alone, saying that his poetry had gained in *"self-possession and power"*.

[17] His later plays included *Crabbed Youth and Age* (1924), which depicts a couple at extreme ends of the age divide; Yeats and George, or Yeats and Lily are not specifically depicted, perhaps because Yeats was the director of his theatre. His play *The Big House* (1926) depicts a burning of a Protestant

manor by Irregulars, or extreme Republicans, and may be a careful revelation of the violence that was being suffered by the Anglo-Irish ruling class, including Yeats, after they had put down by violent means the Catholic underclass over the case of Honor Bright.

[18] Wikipedia: Kevin O'Higgins
[19] David Neligan: *The Spy In The Castle*
[20] Yeats's poem *Meeting* from *A Woman Young and Old* says *Each hating what the other loved, Face to face we stood.* There were obvious political differences between a Catholic shop assistant and an elderly wealthy senator.
[21] The best example of this is *The Tower* series of poems.
[22] He had moved from the United Arts Club on becoming a senator.
[23] Maddox *George's Ghosts* p. 132 George's voices resumed their orders to Yeats regarding his duty to achieve a son.
[24] Maddox p. 220
[25] c.f. *The Mermaid* and *The Death of the Hare* in *A Man Young and Old*.
[26] Such as Senator Rev. Peter Finlay.
[27] The Senate Speeches of W. B. Yeats, p. 92

[28] According to my memories of childhood in the English West Midlands.
[29] According to Breeda MacDonald, who gave me photographs of Michael and his wife.
[30] Possibly Switzers, but there is no evidence for this beyond the claims of journalists.
[31] According to Kilmainham Gaol Museum listings.
[32] These entries are in one series of poems, "A Man Young and Old" which is dealt with in the chapter headed 'Ruin Wreck and Wrack'.
[33] Located in the Liberties, outside the city walls, it is not known who owned this seventeenth century mansion, demolished about 1940, but a local grocery-stall keeper collected the rents.
[34] From 1829 it catered for women too poor to pay for medical care during childbirth.
[35] Calling him Kevin Barry showed dismay at the British hanging of an IRA man at Mountjoy Jail on 1st Nov. 1920, but this was not necessarily political. He was an 18-year-old Protestant medical student from a farming family in Rathvilly, Co. Carlow, unknown to her. The current Kevin Barry agrees with me.
[36] Based on 40 weeks gestation plus 10 days extra for a first-time mother.
[37] Childbirth was not accelerated through use of drugs and surgical techniques common in 2015.
[38] Maddox, George's Ghosts p 159

[39] Ibid
[40] Ibid p. 161
[41] Ibid
[42] *"There were no facilities and a general tendency to criminalise unmarried mothers."* Reviewer: R. McCord to Cliona Rattigan's 'What Else Could I Do?'
[43] WBY to John Quinn, Oct.30 1920, Wade, p. 663. This shows that Yeats had told Quinn and Gogarty about his affair with Lily and her pregnancy and asked for their help.
[44] Ibid p. 163
[45] According to Charles Lynch's Witness Deposition.
[46] Although Irish law did not permit an illegitimate son to inherit, the father could determine otherwise if he so desired.
[47] Biography of Leopold J. Dillon on Wikitree.
[48] Dubliner Peter Yeates states this in his song "Honor Bright", written in 1975 for his band "Full Shilling", based on what his mother used to tell him as a child. She told him everyone knew this.
[49] Dillon's and Purcell's Witness Depositions.
[50] Felix Reilly's Witness Deposition.
[51] Supt. John Reynolds' Witness Deposition.
[52] Wkipedia: Dr J P Brennan
[53] DEM 9th June 1925
[54] See newspapers from 9th June 1925 at Dublin City Library, Pearse St.
[55] DEM 9/6/1925
[56] John Reynolds, son of Supt. John Reynolds, reported to me the arrival of O'Duffy and his father's anger at this shocking event. He said his father thought nothing good could come of this.
[57] At the beginning of my genealogical research Garda Archives sent me a detail not found in newspapers, namely Lily's place of birth. This proved that they still hold evidence not available to the public.

[59] Kevin only found out who his mother actually was much later, when he joined the British Army in 1942; as an Irish volunteer he had to produce his birth certificate to verify his age.
[60] See Appendix 4, scans of the document.
[61] "*Amalthusian sheath*" should read 'A Malthusian sheath', meaning a condom.
[62] Dublin Evening Mail (DEM) 2/2/1926
[63] Ibid.
[64] DEM 30/7/1926 and WD written by Neligan.
Continued on page 143
[66] DEM 1/2/1926

[67] Ibid

[69] Ibid
[70] DEM 2/2/1926
[71] DEM 2.2.1926
[72] Ibid
[73] She had often met Yeats in St Stephens Green, since his clubs and houses were situated there.
[74] DEM18.8.1925
[75] DEM 2/2/1926
[76] Patrick Purcell's Witness Deposition (WD)
[77] Purcell's WD
[78] DEM 3/2/1926
[79] Dillon's Witness Deposition (WD)
[80] Evening Herald (EH) 18/8/1925
[81] Woodruffe's WD
[82] Mike Powell, Artists Rifles Regimental Roll of Honour and War Record 1914-1919, The Federation of Family History Societies, Wikipedia
[83] Ibid
[84] The Secrets of the Old.
[85] Madge Hopkins' witness deposition.
[86] Yeats did know Margaret and James; in *"A Prayer to my Son"* he refers to them in the last verse as *"a woman and a man"*.
[87] Scholars of Yeats have shown that Mrs French and the peasant girl actually did exist in Ireland. However Yeats is using their names and circumstances because his lips have been sealed concerning George or Lily.
[88] Many other poems show Yeats's grief from 1925 until his death in 1939. I am quoting the most obvious ones.

[89] Also known as 'Peg and Meg' (like Madge and Margery, two more diminutives of Margaret) in another poem.

[90] Collected Poems: W B Yeats. 1909-62, ed. D. Albright, p.204
[91] The English Auden, p. 391
[92] Introduction to The Poems: W. B. Yeats ed. D. Albright p. lvi.
[93] George added the extra *'s'* at the end of "*...mocker...*" to obscure the meaning.
[94] Despite the contemporary fashion of living with your child during its early years, this was not accepted practise in the 1920s. As in Victorian times children were not acceptable in adult society until they were able to behave well, so that many well-to-do children were farmed out for the first decade

(approximately) to hired carers.

[95] Lists of political members at Kilmainham Jail Museum, Cumann na Bhann, Sinn Fein etc. have been carefully checked for all three of Lily's names. She was not in any such groups.

[96] Maud Gonne to W. B. Yeats, October 1927, quoted by Brenda Maddox in *Yeats' Ghosts*, p. 244

[97] From www.boards.ie

[98] *"...Kevin O'Higgins countenance...wears /A gentle questioning look that cannot hide /A soul incapable of remorse or rest..." from 'The Municipal Gallery Revisited' by W B Yeats.*

[99] So said my mother.

[100] León Ó Broin, 'Frank Duff, A Biography' Gill & Macmillan 1982, p. 1-5

[101] Montgomery Street ('the Monto') was the prostitution area, northwest of the river Liffey. Francis Street and Newmarket were southeast of the river.

[102] Ibid p 17

[103] Ibid p.21

[104] This did stick in the public mind with deleterious effects. A famous professor immediately dismissed my theory of an affair beween her and Yeats with an airy "Oh, the *legendary* Honor Bright!"

[105] She attended Ballon National School until the age of fourteen and got average or higher marks.

[106] There is no evidence of this.

[107] All quotes on pp 245 to 248 are from Finegan pp. 7-10.

www.ingramcontent.com/pod-product-compliance
Lightning Source LLC
Chambersburg PA
CBHW050806160426
43192CB00010B/1663